SOCCER MADE SIMPLE:
A SPECTATOR'S GUIDE

by Dave Ominsky and P.J. Harari

Cover design and illustrations by Eugene Cheltenham

Photographs © by
Allsport Photography and Bruce Bennett Studios

Look for these other Spectator Guides:

- Baseball Made Simple
- Basketball Made Simple
- Football Made Simple
- Ice Hockey Made Simple
- Olympics Made Simple

ISBN 1-884309-01-1
Library of Congress Catalog Card Number: 94-94164

We welcome your comments and questions:
FIRST BASE SPORTS, INC.
P.O. BOX 1731
MANHATTAN BEACH, CALIFORNIA 90267-1731
U.S.A.
(310) 318-3006

Photographs provided in this publication are for editorial illustration only and do not indicate any affiliation between the publishers of this book and World Cup 1994, FIFA, USSF, or any teams or players.

HOW TO USE THIS BOOK

Soccer has a global following unrivaled by any other sport. It is played by an estimated 100 million people worldwide and is also the fastest growing sport played by American youths, both male and female. Now, with the United States hosting the World Cup in 1994, the number of soccer fans is set to grow by leaps and bounds.

This book aims to educate anyone who wants to know more about this exciting international game. It is written for use by a variety of audiences — adults who want to become fans, children who want to learn the basics of the sport they are playing and even existing fans who want a quick reference guide to their favorite sport.

Each chapter has been written to stand alone, so you do not have to sit and read the book from cover to cover. However, the chapters do build on each other, so if you start at page 1 and read through to the end, the chapters flow logically and become more detailed as you progress.

This book will mainly discuss soccer rules as established for international play by FIFA's 17 Laws of the Game. However, as the sport is played at so many different levels, from youth to college to professional leagues, this book will also outline the differences when they are important. The Laws are not reprinted in this book because they are not organized to allow for quick reference and contain many details that are not important to your enjoyment of the game. However, they have been rewritten by the authors of this Spectator's Guide to be easier to use.

Rules, as well as any word or phrase printed in *italics*, can be referenced quickly and easily using the book's glossary or index. So get ready to learn about the sport that has attracted such a huge international following.

SOCCER ORGANIZATIONS

Many soccer organizations exist worldwide to govern the game in individual countries. The most important organizations to soccer in the U.S. are:

FIFA (Federation Internationale de Football Association)
Established in 1904 and based in Zurich, Switzerland, FIFA is the official governing body of international soccer. FIFA sponsors the *World Cup* (the championship of soccer held every 4 years), helps establish and update the official rules of the game (called the 17 *Laws of the Game*) and releases rankings of its 178 member national teams. It is FIFA that imposes sanctions and penalties against players or teams who display poor conduct in international competition.

IFAB (International Football Association Board)
This organization approves all changes in the Laws of the Game. Composed of 4 British soccer organizations and FIFA, it meets annually to update and refine these rules.

USSF (United States Soccer Federation)
Formed in 1913, this organization governs soccer in the U.S. The USSF is America's link to FIFA, providing soccer rules and guidelines to players, *referees* and spectators nationwide.

USYSA (United States Youth Soccer Association)
The official Youth Division of the USSF, the USYSA is comprised of 55 state soccer associations across America, and is the largest youth soccer organization in the U.S. with nearly 2 million registered members. It organizes and administers youth league competitions, establishes rules and guidelines, and holds clinics and workshops to support players, coaches and referees.

AYSO (American Youth Soccer Organization)
AYSO is another administrative body of youth soccer, providing information and equipment to youth league referees, coaches and players. AYSO has adopted most of its

rules from FIFA but has also made changes to improve the game for youth league play.

NCAA (National Collegiate Athletic Association) Soccer Committee

One of the NCAA's many committees, it establishes rules and guidelines for collegiate-level soccer. Its rules once differed radically from FIFA's international rules, but today only a few minor differences remain.

CONCACAF (Confederation Norte-Centroamericana y Del Caribe de Football)

This is the regional organization of North American and Central American soccer under which World Cup *qualifying matches* are played. Member countries include the U.S., Canada and Mexico, as well as many Central American and Caribbean countries. In the past few World Cups, FIFA has invited the top 2 or 3 teams from this conference to compete in the tournament.

APSL (American Professional Soccer League)

Founded in 1990 and sanctioned by the USSF, this is the only major outdoor professional soccer league playing in the U.S. today. It consists of 8 teams in the U.S. and Canada (expanding to 12 by 1995) and plays its games in the spring and summer. The league follows the FIFA Laws of the Game.

NPSL (National Professional Soccer League)

This U.S. indoor soccer league uses modified soccer rules and plays in hockey rinks adapted for soccer. Points are assigned in a multiple scoring system like basketball, with 1, 2 and 3-point plays. It consists of 12 teams and plays its games from October through April.

MLS (Major League Soccer)

This proposed new outdoor league is scheduled to begin play in the Spring of 1995. Headed by USSF President *Alan Rothenberg*, MLS intends to establish 12 teams under centralized ownership. A rule requiring that most players be American-born is expected to instill greater national interest.

TABLE OF CONTENTS

THE ORIGINS OF SOCCER

THE BEGINNING

Called *football* everywhere in the world except in the United States, soccer is the oldest known team sport. Historians are not sure exactly where soccer began, but some form of kicking game has been played by man for thousands of years. A game called "tsu chu" was played by the Chinese over 2,500 years ago where participants tried to kick a leather ball filled with hair between bamboo poles. The ancient Romans and Greeks also played a kicking game using a cow's bladder filled with air.

The sport first attained widespread popularity in the British Islands. It was the Romans who brought their violent kicking game (called "harpastum") there during the 3rd century. Several hundred years later, in the 9th century, when invading Danish warriors were defeated by British reinforcements and beheaded, triumphant villagers kicked the heads around in celebration. By the 11th century, kicking games had become more organized, with entire villages competing against each other on mile-long fields for many hours at a time. Their games were extremely violent affairs where players would kick, trip and otherwise maul each other. Players often sustained broken bones and other injuries.

The games became so violent that all forms of kicking games were banned in England by several different kings, but the bans were difficult to enforce because too many people ignored them. In the 16th century, the first versions of organized soccer were played in some Italian towns. Organized games spread across Europe, and in 1624, the first intercollegiate soccer games were played by English schools such as Eton, Winchester and Rugby. Each school chose its own set of rules to play by, with differences in such areas as field size and the number of players on a team.

THE BATTLE BETWEEN SOCCER AND RUGBY

It was not until the 1800s that an effort was made to establish consistent rules for soccer. It began with an incident at Rugby

College in 1823. During a soccer match, William Ellis, a student there, became frustrated by his inability to advance the ball with his feet, so he picked it up and ran with it. While clearly against the rules of most versions of soccer, some players liked the idea of carrying the ball, and the sport of *rugby* was born.

Opponents of this new version of the game, who were anxious to avoid such radical change, sensed an urgency to set standardized rules. In 1846 at Cambridge University, the first complete set of official soccer rules were written. These rules formally outlawed tripping, *holding* and *hacking* (kicking an opponent's legs) which at one time had all been acceptable tactics. In the ensuing years, as rugby became more popular, soccer traditionalists tried to make the separation clearer. In 1863, the *English Football Association* was formed to govern future rule changes.

It was this split between the two sports that actually led to the use of "soccer" instead of "football" as the name of the game today in the United States. To distinguish between the two versions (original football versus rugby), people began to call the kicking-only game "association football" after the English Football Association. Association was abbreviated by "assoc." which eventually led to it being called "soccer football". When the sport was brought to the U.S., the name "soccer" stuck. (See chapter entitled **SOCCER IN THE U.S.**)

Because of the influence of the British Empire in the 19th century, soccer spread quickly, first across Europe, and then to South America and Asia. In 1904, the *Federation Internationale de Football Association* (*FIFA*) was established in Paris by the 7 European countries of France, Belgium, Denmark, the Netherlands, Spain, Sweden and Switzerland. The purpose of FIFA was to become the governing body of soccer around the world, giving it the right to organize a world championship for soccer. This was the beginning of the *World Cup*.

OBJECT OF THE GAME

Soccer is a fast-paced game played on a large grass *field* by two teams of 11 players each. Players try to maneuver a ball into the opponent's *net* to score *points*, called *goals*. The object of the game is for each team to try to score more goals than its opponent. Soccer is unique in that it is the only major sport where players may not use their hands or arms to touch the ball. The players may use any other part of their body, including their feet, legs, head and chest.

The one player on each team who is allowed to use his hands and arms to control the ball is the *goalkeeper* or *goalie* because of the difficulty of the task he faces. The goalie's job is to stand in front of his team's goal and prevent any shots from getting into the net behind him.

Soccer is a sport of constant motion, and a *match* can be stopped only by the *referee* under certain circumstances. If a player needs a rest or sustains a minor injury, the game continues without waiting for him. In fact, most of the rules are quite logical, stemming from two overall concerns: the desire to keep the game moving and to protect players from serious injury. If you keep these two ideas in mind, you will have little trouble understanding the rules of the game.

THE 17 LAWS OF SOCCER

Unlike many other sports that have hundreds of rules, soccer's official regulations are broken down into 17 main sections, called the *Laws of the Game*. These Laws are established by *FIFA* and changes are approved annually at an *IFAB* meeting held in February or March.

The authors have reorganized the Laws in this Spectator's Guide so that they will be easier to use. They are not referred to again by their official numbers, but you can find the chapter in which a particular law is discussed by using the index or the table below:

TABLE 1: FIFA's 17 LAWS OF THE GAME

#	LAW	OUR CHAPTER*
I	THE FIELD OF PLAY	THE SOCCER FIELD
II	THE BALL	UNIFORMS & EQUIPMENT
III	NUMBER OF PLAYERS	HOW THE GAME IS PLAYED
IV	PLAYERS' EQUIPMENT	UNIFORMS & EQUIPMENT
V	REFEREES	THE OFFICIALS
VI	LINESMEN	THE OFFICIALS
VII	DURATION OF THE GAME	HOW THE GAME IS PLAYED
VIII	THE START OF PLAY	HOW THE GAME IS PLAYED
IX	BALL IN AND OUT OF PLAY	HOW THE GAME IS PLAYED
X	METHOD OF SCORING	HOW THE GAME IS PLAYED
XI	OFF-SIDE	OFFSIDE RULE
XII	FOULS AND MISCONDUCT	FOULS
XIII	FREE-KICK	HOW THE GAME IS PLAYED/FOULS
XIV	PENALTY-KICK	HOW THE GAME IS PLAYED/FOULS
XV	THROW-IN	HOW THE GAME IS PLAYED
XVI	GOAL-KICK	HOW THE GAME IS PLAYED
XVII	CORNER-KICK	HOW THE GAME IS PLAYED

* Please check the **INDEX** for other chapters where the subjects may also be discussed

There are only 5 general areas where FIFA allows the rules to be altered for younger players (under 16 years old), veteran players (over 35) or women. These areas are:

- Size of the field
- Size, weight or material of the ball
- Dimensions of the *goal*
- Length of the *periods*
- Number of *substitutions*

More detail is provided later in the chapter on **YOUTH LEAGUE DIFFERENCES**.

THE SOCCER FIELD

The place where soccer *matches* are played is called a *field* or *pitch*. The field is a large rectangular area with dimensions specified by the rules of the governing body at each level. Every field has two *goals*, one at each end, and white lines are painted on the grass to define important areas where the rules of play are enforced.

According to *FIFA*, the field must fall within a range of sizes. The length must be between 100 and 130 yards (110-120 yards for international and collegiate matches), and the width between 50 and 100 yards (70-80 international, 65-80 college). (See **Figure 1**) The width must be less than the length to create a rectangular shape. One of the more common sizes is 110 x 70 yards. The field is bounded on all sides by an *out-of-bounds* line, no more than 5 inches thick. A ball that completely crosses this line anytime during the game is considered out of bounds or *out of play*. (See **Figure 2**) When this happens, play stops temporarily and is quickly restarted by a player who puts the ball back inside one of these lines, or back *in play*. There are two types of out-of-bounds lines on a soccer field: *sidelines* and *goal lines*.

- Sidelines: Also called *touchlines*, these lines run along the length of the field on each side. When a ball completely crosses one of these lines, the game is stopped and restarted by a *throw-in*.

- Goal Lines: Also called *endlines*, these lines run along the width of the field at each end. They run across the *goalmouth*, the opening to each goal. When a ball completely crosses one of these lines, but does not go into the goal, the game is stopped and restarted by a *goal kick* or *corner kick*, depending on which team knocked the ball out of bounds.

Throw-ins, goal kicks and corner kicks are discussed further in the chapter **HOW THE GAME IS PLAYED**.

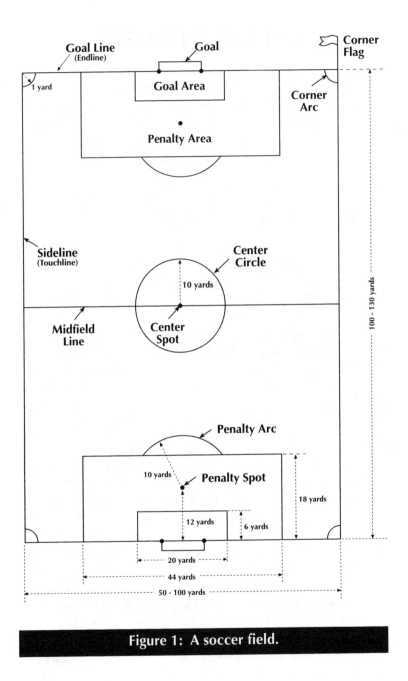

Figure 1: A soccer field.

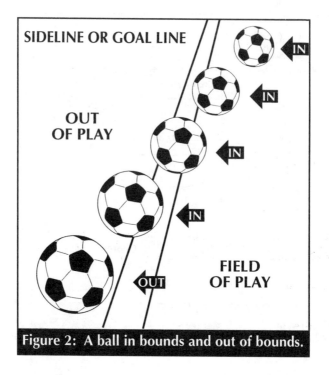

Figure 2: A ball in bounds and out of bounds.

SIDELINE OR GOAL LINE

OUT OF PLAY

IN
IN
IN
IN
OUT

FIELD OF PLAY

THE GOAL

Centered on each goal line is a goal, shown in **Figure 3**. It is constructed of a wooden or metal frame that consists of two vertical *goalposts* anchored in the ground and a horizontal *crossbar* that sits on top of the posts. The frame is 24 feet wide by 8 feet high and must be painted white. A ball must pass through this opening to score a goal. A *net*, made of hemp, jute or nylon cord is draped over the frame and extends behind the goal, either fastened to the ground or attached to a part of the frame that also extends backward. The net is needed so that a ball cannot pass through the opening without being recognized as a goal. The words "net" and "goal" are used interchangeably.

The goal is very important as this is where all the scoring occurs. The winner of the game is determined solely by which team can put more balls across the goal line and into the goal.

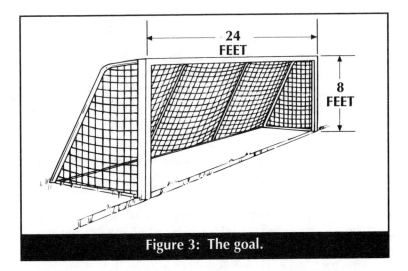

Figure 3: The goal.

OTHER AREAS

On the field, there are several other areas defined with white lines where other rules apply. The following 3 areas are at each end:

- *Penalty Area*: A rectangular area 44 yards wide by 18 yards deep, with its long edge on the goal line. This is the only area in which a *goalkeeper* may use his hands to block or control the ball. Outside this box, a *goalie* who touches the ball with his hands is subject to a *foul* like any other player.

- *Goal Area*: A rectangular area 20 yards wide by 6 yards deep which lies within the penalty area and has its long edge on the goal line. Inside this area, the rules protect the goalie by making it illegal for opposing players to bump (or *charge*) him. Also, all goal kicks are taken from inside this box.

- *Penalty Spot*: A small circular spot located 12 yards in front of the center of the goal line and at the center of the *penalty arc*. It is from this spot that all *penalty kicks* are taken. Penalty kicks are explained in the chapter entitled **HOW THE GAME IS PLAYED**.

- Penalty Arc: An arc drawn with a 10 yard radius from the penalty spot. It designates an area that opposing players are not allowed to enter prior to a penalty kick.

These other areas are also designated by white lines on the field:

- *Corner Arc*: A quarter-circle with a 1 yard radius located in each of the 4 corners of the field from which all corner kicks are taken. There is a *corner flag* inside each corner arc.

- *Center Circle*: A circle with a 10 yard radius centered in the middle of the field which is used on *kickoffs* that start or restart the game. All players except the one kicking off must remain outside this circle until play has started.

- *Center Spot*: A small circular mark at the center of the field and inside the *center circle* on which the ball is placed when a kickoff is taken to start or restart the game.

- *Midfield Line*: A line that divides the field in half along its width, also called the *center line*. When a kickoff is taken, all players on a team must be standing on the side of this line that contains the goal they are defending.

TAKING SIDES

In war, a country's territory is that land which they occupy and defend. The situation is similar in soccer, where a team's *territory* is considered to be the area that it defends. This is why the half of the field containing the goal that a team is defending is called "their own side" and the goal called "their own goal".

Now that you are familiar with the layout of the soccer field, let us take a look at the uniforms worn and equipment used to play on it.

UNIFORMS & EQUIPMENT

THE SOCCER BALL

A soccer ball is a black and white checkered sphere made of leather, vinyl or other materials approved by the governing organization at each level. It must measure between 27 and 28 inches in circumference and weigh between 14 and 16 ounces. The ball is inflated with air at a pressure of 0.6-1.1 atmospheres (8.8 to 16.2 pounds per square inch). It cannot be changed during the game unless the *referee* authorizes it.

PLAYER UNIFORMS & EQUIPMENT

The equipment used by soccer players is among the most simple and least expensive of any sport, greatly contributing to soccer's international popularity. Most soccer players simply wear a shirt, shorts, shoes, socks and *shinguards*. *Goalies* must wear a different-colored jersey from the other players and the referee so they can be easily identified. No player's shoes can have any feature that might cause another player harm, such as exposed metal spikes. However, rubber or plastic *cleats* are legal. (See **Figure 4**) The only protection players may wear are shinguards, knee pads and elbow pads.

On the back of each player's uniform, there is a number to identify him to the officials and spectators. The numbers are usually assigned in a systematic order, with the goalie wearing #1, defensive players wearing the next higher numbers, followed by the offensive players and finally the substitutes.

Legal   **Illegal**

Figure 4: Soccer shoes.

HOW THE GAME IS PLAYED

Ten of the 11 players on each team run up and down the *field* trying to score *goals* by maneuvering the ball into their opponent's *net*, while at the same time trying to prevent the opposing team from scoring. The 11th player is the *goalkeeper* who stays near his team's goal to protect it. The team that has scored the most goals by the end of the game is the winner.

GOALS

In soccer, a goal is scored when the entire ball crosses the *goal line* between the two *goalposts* and below the *crossbar*, whether it is on the ground or in the air. A goal is not allowed if the ball was touched by the hands or arms of a player on the team that scored. In soccer, goals are difficult to score (often only 1 or 2 per game for each team) so each is considered very valuable.

OFFENSE AND DEFENSE

The team that has control of the ball is said to have *possession* of the ball, and is known as the *offensive team* or *attacking team* (*on offense*). It uses *dribbling* and *passing* to advance it towards the opposing team's goal, and tries to *score* by *shooting* it at the goal.

The team that does not have the ball is called the *defensive* or *defending team* (*on defense*). It tries to prevent the attacking team from scoring by *marking* (following closely) and *tackling* (trying to dislodge the ball from) *attacking players*. Dribbling, passing, shooting, marking and tackling will all be discussed in the chapter entitled **PLAYER SKILLS**.

Possession switches from Team A to Team B whenever Team A scores a goal or commits a *turnover* in one of the following ways:

- Team B *steals* the ball
- Team A makes a bad pass
- Team A knocks the ball *out of bounds*
- Team A is called for a *foul*

As soon as possession of the ball switches from one team to the other, the attacking team becomes the defense, and the defending team becomes the offense. The roles of offense and defense switch constantly throughout a game.

LENGTH OF THE GAME

According to *FIFA* rules for international play, a *regulation game* consists of two 45-minute *halves* or *periods* with a 5-minute *intermission* or *halftime* in between (10 minutes in college). Most games played in youth leagues have shorter periods. After intermission, the teams switch ends of the field so that each team is now defending the goal it attacked during the first half.

There is usually an unofficial game clock visible to fans attending a soccer *match* showing the time remaining in a period; however, the official time is kept only by the *referee* who holds the *official game clock*. Neither clock stops at any time during the game, not even when play is stopped. However, when play stops for an injury or if a team tries to waste time, the referee counts this time and adds it to the official game clock, extending the end of the period. This is called *injury time* and is why any period may continue even after the unofficial game clock has expired. The length of a period can also be extended to permit a *penalty kick* after the official time has expired. Penalty kicks will be explained later in this chapter.

According to *NCAA* collegiate rules, the *timekeeper* does temporarily stop the clock in 5 situations, when:

- A goal is scored
- A penalty kick is awarded
- A player receives a *yellow card* or *red card*
- A television *timeout* is called
- The referee signals a stoppage for any reason

TIES, OVERTIME & TIEBREAKERS

When a regulation game ends with an equal number of goals having been scored by each team, the game is a *tie game*. In regular international competition, the game ends tied and it is called a *draw*. However, in some matches, tie-breaking procedures are used to determine a winner. In international championship contests, for example, where a winner *must* be declared to determine a champion, a full 30-minutes of *overtime* is played in two 15-minute periods after regulation. Teams switch sides between periods. The team with the most goals at the end of the extra periods wins. If the game is still tied after the overtime periods, the match is decided by a *tiebreaker*.

At the collegiate level, the two extra 15-minute periods are always played at the end of a tied game, whether or not a winner needs to be decided. If a *regular-season* game is still tied after that, it ends in a draw. However, if a winner must be chosen, the game is decided by a tiebreaker (but only after two additional 15-minute *sudden-death* overtime periods are played if neither team has a game scheduled the next day).

A tiebreaker is a series of penalty kicks or *penalty shots* taken by players from both teams. Only players who were on the field at the end of the overtime period are eligible to participate. A coin toss decides which team kicks first. Then, the teams alternate turns taking penalty shots at one goal defended by the opposing goalie, and a different shooter must take each shot until a team runs out of eligible players. Eligible players may then get a second shot. After 5 shots by each team, the team with the most goals wins the game. If the teams have made the same number of shots out of 5, they continue to take shots one-by-one until one team scores and the other does not, thereby deciding the match.

STARTING PLAY

A soccer match is started with a *kickoff* in which a player passes the ball forward to a teammate from the *center spot*. Prior to this kickoff, each team must remain completely in its own *territory*, and players from the defending team must also stay outside the *center circle*. The ball must go forward one full rotation to be considered *in play*.

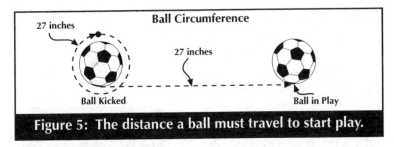

Figure 5: The distance a ball must travel to start play.

A coin flip before the game gives the winner of the toss a choice: to kickoff, or to select which side of the field it wants to defend. If a team decides to kickoff, the loser of the toss gets to choose which side to defend. To start the second half, the two teams switch ends of the field, and the team that did not kickoff to start the game now kicks off.

A kickoff also restarts the game after each goal. The team that allowed the goal kicks off.

STOPPING PLAY

Whenever the ball is considered *out of play* by an *official*, the referee temporarily stops the game but not the game clock. A ball is out of play as soon as the whole of the ball has crossed over the entire width of a *sideline* or *goal line*, whether it is rolling on the ground or flying through the air. (See **Figure 2** in the chapter **THE SOCCER FIELD**) The position of a player who might be touching the ball is irrelevant — only the position of the ball matters. (See **Figure 6**) A ball is also considered out of play whenever the referee stops play for any other reason, such as for the assessment of a *foul* or for a serious injury. A ball is

15

considered still in play even if it hits the goalposts or the referee, as long as the ball does not cross one of the *out-of-bounds* lines.

RESTARTING PLAY

After each stoppage of play, the game is restarted by a player from the team opposing the one that caused the stoppage. If Team A last touched the ball before it went out of bounds or if one of its players committed a foul, Team B restarts the game. Play is restarted in different ways — by a *throw-in, goal kick, corner kick, drop ball, free kick* or *penalty kick* — depending on how the

Figure 6: Ball is in bounds even if player is out of bounds.

stoppage occurred. **Table 2** illustrates when each type of restart is used. A diagram showing the path of the ball for some of these restart methods is shown in **Figure 7**. In

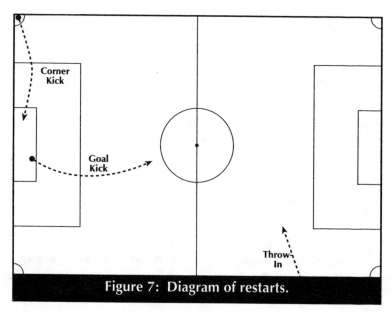

Figure 7: Diagram of restarts.

TABLE 2: STOPPAGES AND RESTARTS

TYPE OF STOPPAGE	RESTART METHOD
Ball crosses sideline	Throw-In
Ball crosses goal line, last touched by offense	Goal Kick by Defense
Ball crosses goal line, last touched by defense	Corner Kick by Offense
Non-serious foul	Indirect Free Kick
More serious foul	Direct Free Kick
Most serious foul or foul by defense in penalty area	Penalty Kick
Injury or uncertainty	Drop Ball

each case, just as in a kickoff, the ball is not considered to be back in play until it has traveled one full rotation (as shown earlier in **Figure 5**).

TYPES OF STOPPAGES / RESTARTS
Throw-In
If the ball crosses one of the sidelines, play is stopped and a throw-in restarts the action. (See **Figure 8**) If Team A caused play to stop, a player from Team B tosses the ball over his head with two hands back into the field. The

player must be facing the field with both feet on the ground, either on or behind the sideline, at the point where the ball went out of bounds. He may move his feet prior to the throw but cannot lift them off the ground during or immediately after the throw.

If a ball is improperly thrown, such as with only one hand or with one of the thrower's feet leaving the ground, a violation is called and a throw-in is taken by

Figure 8: Throw-in.

a player from the other team. If the thrower tries to *play* the ball (i.e., touch the ball in any way) before another player touches it, an *indirect free kick* is taken by the opposing team. Free kicks are discussed later in this chapter.

<u>Goal Kick or Corner Kick</u>
When the ball crosses over the goal line without entering the goal, the officials note the last team to touch the ball to determine how the game is restarted. If a member of the attacking team last touched the ball, the defending team gets to take a goal kick. However, if the defense last touched the ball, the offense restarts play with a corner kick, a potent offensive weapon.

In a goal kick, any member of the team that was on defense places the ball inside the *goal area* in front of his goal. It is placed in the left or right half of the goal area nearest to where the ball crossed the goal line. No opposing player may be inside the *penalty area*. The player then kicks the ball away from his own goal to restart play. (See **Figure 7**) The ball is not in play until it has left the penalty area, and even the kicker's teammates must wait until it is in play to touch it, or the kick must be retaken. Like a throw-in, the kicker may not play the ball again until another player has touched it.

A corner kick is an excellent chance for a team to score because it allows the attacking team to bring many of its offensive players into an area in front of the opposition's net. In a corner kick, a member of the attacking team places the ball in the *corner area* nearest to where the ball crossed the goal line. Players from both teams gather in front of the goal in anticipation of a kick into that area. The kicker then tries to kick the ball directly into the goal or to one of his teammates, hopefully giving that teammate the chance to deflect the ball into the goal. (See **Figure 7**) No player from the opposing team may get within 10 yards of the kicker until the ball is back in play. Like a throw-in, the kicker may not play the ball again until another player has touched it.

Free Kick or Penalty Kick
When the referee calls a *foul* against a player, he stops play and orders it restarted by either a free kick or a penalty kick, depending on the severity of the violation. There are two types of free kicks — direct and indirect. In each, a player from the non-offending team places the ball on the ground at the spot of the rule violation and kicks it free of any players closer than 10 yards. The kicker may not touch the ball again until another player has.

When a non-serious foul is called against a player from Team A, Team B takes an *indirect free kick*. "Indirect" means that the player taking the free kick cannot score directly on the kick. Instead, another player must touch the ball before a goal can be scored. If Team A commits the foul inside its own goal area, Team B repositions the ball on the edge of the goal area furthest from the goal (the side parallel to the goal line) to take the indirect free kick.

A *direct free kick* is awarded for more severe violations of the rules. Since a goal may be scored right from a direct free kick, one taken by an attacking team near its opponent's goal is an excellent *scoring opportunity*.

Since free kicks are taken at the spot where the foul was committed, a foul by the defending team near its own goal gives the attacking team a free kick at close range to the goal. To protect their goal from such a close kick, the defenders are allowed to form a *wall* of players between the kicker and their goalie. (See **Figure 9**) This wall, consisting of players squeezed shoulder-to-shoulder, creates a more difficult shot by reducing the area of open goal at which the kicker has to shoot. The number of players used ranges from 2 to 6 and depends on the

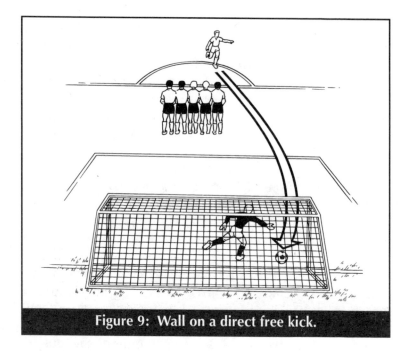

Figure 9: Wall on a direct free kick.

strategy chosen by the defending team. The wall must be at least 10 yards from the kicker unless the players in the wall cannot stay this distance and still fit on the field (such as when a free kick is taken within 10 yards of the goal); in this case, they may stand on their own goal line between the goalposts.

For the most severe infractions or those committed by the defense in its own penalty area, the non-offending team is awarded a penalty kick, one of the most exciting plays in soccer. (See **Figure 10**) This play, also called a *penalty shot* or *penalty* for short, is a one-on-one confrontation between the goalie of the offending team and a player chosen by the opposition as its kicker. All other players must remain outside the *penalty area* and *penalty arc*, at least 10 yards from the kicker. For penalty kicks taken in a tiebreaker, all other players must remain within the center circle.

The kicker places the ball on the *penalty spot* and attempts to kick the ball past the goalie. He must play the ball

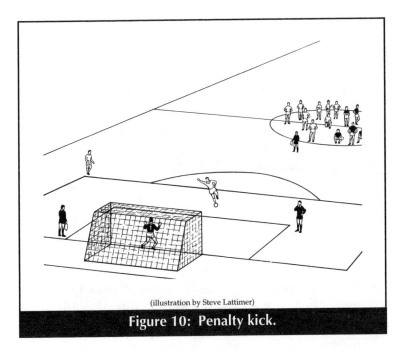

(illustration by Steve Lattimer)

Figure 10: Penalty kick.

forward and may not touch the ball again until another player has, or the opposition is awarded an indirect free kick. This means that he can play a rebound off the goalie but not off the goalposts or crossbar. (In a tiebreaker, the kick is over as soon as the ball stops moving forward). The goalie must stand on the goal line and is not allowed to move his feet before the ball is kicked or the kicker gets to take another penalty shot (if he missed the first shot). In professional play, kickers almost always score on penalty kicks. If a goalie hopes to stop a good penalty shot, he must guess correctly where the ball will go and move quickly as soon as it is kicked.

Drop Ball
In all other cases where the officials stop play, a drop ball is used to restart the game; for example, if the ball becomes deflated, if 2 opposing players commit similar fouls or if play is stopped because of injury. To restart play, the referee drops the ball between 2 opposing players, each facing the other's goal, at the last location on the field that

the ball was in play. Neither player can touch the ball until it touches the ground.

SUBSTITUTIONS

Substitutions for players on the field can be made only during a stoppage of play, and only after the referee has given a gesture to the entering player to do so. Substitution rules vary according to the level of competition. Compared with other team sports, soccer at the international level permits very few substitutions. For example, *World Cup* rules allow only 2 substitutions per match for whatever reason, and once a player is replaced he may not play again for the rest of the game. In fact, it was not until 1970 that World Cup rules allowed any substitutions, even for injuries. Before the rule was changed, an injured player could either attempt to continue playing or choose not to play, forcing his team to play one man short, or *shorthanded*, for the remainder of the game.

Naturally, coaches prefer to save these 2 substitutions to replace players who might get seriously injured later in the match, and sometimes they are not used at all. To conserve his team's substitutions, a player who sustains a minor injury or who needs minor equipment repairs may simply leave the field temporarily without being substituted for while his team plays shorthanded. Such a player may then re-enter the game at any stoppage of play with the referee's permission.

The rationale behind the strict replacement rules at the international level is to reward soccer players for having the stamina to stay in the game without any rest. In contrast, substitution rules at the collegiate and youth levels generally allow for substitutes to leave and enter the game freely with no limit to the total number of changes. For example, in college games, substitutions may be made any time the ball crosses the goal line or when an injury occurs, although substituted players may re-enter the game only during the second half. At the youth level, players who are replaced are permitted to re-enter between periods or at their midway points. Many traditional fans remain critical of these liberalized substitution rules, citing that players have less need to pace themselves if they know they can rest on the sidelines.

At any level of play, a player who is ejected by the referee may not be replaced, and his team must play shorthanded for the remainder of the match. Any player on the field may also switch places with the goalie during a stoppage of play after giving the referee notice of the change. This is not counted as an official substitution because the same players remain on the field.

The next chapter entitled **PLAYER SKILLS** describes the wide range of talents soccer players require.

PLAYER SKILLS

OFFENSIVE SKILLS

Soccer players must have many diverse skills that allow them to move the ball up the *field* and score *goals*. Three essential skills are *dribbling*, *passing* and *shooting*.

Dribbling

The basic skill of advancing the ball with the feet while controlling it is called dribbling. A dribbling player touches the ball with his feet just enough to maintain control of the ball's movement while he is running. (See **Figure 11**) Good dribblers can dribble while running almost at full speed. Also important is the ability to *fake*

Figure 11: Dribbling.

out a *defender* by pretending to dribble one way and actually going the other, allowing the dribbler to get around the defender.

When a player controls the ball by dribbling, he and his team is said to *possess* or have *possession* of the ball. Possession is important because players with the ball can pass it among themselves to keep it away from their opponents and move it closer to the opponent's *goal*.

Passing

Passing is when one player kicks the ball to another teammate. It is used to move the ball closer to the opposing goal, to keep the ball away from an opponent or to give the ball to a player who is in a better position to score. Some of the different types of passes that a player can use are:

- *Push Pass*: A player simply pushes the ball with the inside of his foot to another player. This is the most frequently used pass and is the most accurate to a teammate in close to medium range (within 30 yards).

- *Chip Pass*: The passer *lofts* the ball into the air with his foot to a teammate. This is used primarily to evade a defender by kicking the ball over his head.

- *Back Pass*: A pass backwards off the heel of a player's foot to a teammate running behind, or *trailing* him. This allows the passer to *penetrate* the defense (i.e., get behind some of them) and receive a pass deeper in opposition *territory*.

Shooting

Perhaps the most important skill that an *offensive player* can master is shooting — kicking the ball at the opponent's *net* in an attempt to score a goal. Without good shooting skills, a team that dribbles and passes well might never score. Good shooters do not kick the ball unnecessarily hard, but try to control their power for maximum accuracy. To create *scoring opportunities* in many different situations, *attacking players* need to master a variety of shots:

- *Instep Drive*: A shot taken with the instep of a player's foot that usually goes fairly straight; generally considered the most powerful and accurate.

- *Chip Shot*: A shot used to get the ball past the *goalie* by sending it over him. It can be effective when a goalie comes out in front of his net to *cut off the angle* of the shooter.

- *Banana Kick*: Named after the curved trajectory of the ball, this shot enables the shooter to get the ball around the *goalkeeper*. Spin placed on the ball by the shooter causes it to *hook*, or travel from right to left when kicked by a player's right foot (left to right for left-footed kicks), confusing the goalie into being out of position to stop the shot.

- *Volley*: Any ball that a player shoots while it is off the ground. Since the ball usually does not come perfectly to a player's feet, but instead is often bouncing around, there are numerous chances to use this kind of shot during a game. Players who have excellent timing and coordination can turn a mid-air pass or a bouncing ball into a shot at the goal and a good scoring opportunity.

- *Bicycle Kick*: Also known as the *scissors kick*, this is the most acrobatic and dangerous type of volley, where a player kicks the ball in mid-air backward and over his own head, usually making contact above waist level. (See **Figure 12**) A goalkeeper may have difficulty stopping one of these shots since the shooter's back is turned to him, obscuring the ball until the last moment. The bicycle kick is dangerous because the shooter could kick another player in the head.

Figure 12: Bicycle kick.

BALL CONTROL SKILLS

During a soccer game, the ball often seems to bounce around as if it has a mind of its own, moving at a variety of heights, directions and speeds. In order for a player to find opportunities to pass to his teammates and shoot at the goal, he must be skilled at controlling the ball with all parts of his body except his arms and hands. *Heading* and *trapping* are two such skills that, when mastered, make ball control look easy.

Figure 13: Header.

Heading

When a player uses his head to hit the ball, it is called a *header*. (See **Figure 13**) It can be used both as an offensive and defensive weapon. Since the ball is often well above foot level when a player wants to kick it, the header is an important method for striking the ball with both power and accuracy. It is used to shoot at the goal, pass to teammates or get the ball away from a player's own net to prevent a scoring opportunity by his opponent.

Any part of the head can be used to redirect the ball, but most good headers are struck with the forehead (the flattest part) which provides greater ball control. Several different types of headers are described below:

- *Front Header*: The most common type of header, struck by the forehead to travel forward with great power.

- *Back Header*: The head is used to direct the ball backward; especially popular in front of the goal to send a pass or *corner kick* back to an *open* shooter.

- *Flick Header*: A snap of the neck is used to deflect the ball off the side of the head.

- *Diving Header*: This is the only header played on a ball near ground level, where a player throws himself at the ball to quickly shoot, pass or clear it away from his goal; used when a player does not have enough time to get into position to kick it.

Trapping

Trapping is when a player uses his body to slow down or stop a moving ball to better control it. He can then direct it where he wants to by dribbling, passing or shooting. Players most often use their chest, thighs or feet to trap the soccer ball:

- *Chest Trap*: Used to direct a high ball downward so a player can then play it with his feet. (See **Figure 14**)

Figure 14: Chest trap.

- *Thigh Trap*: Used to control a ball that is in the air but below a player's chest.

- *Foot Trap*: The bottom or sides of a player's shoe are used to control a rolling or low-bouncing ball.

DEFENSIVE SKILLS
Good defense is when defenders are able to prevent the opposition from scoring, without committing *fouls*. Two main skills utilized by defensive players are *marking* and *tackling*.

Marking
Marking is just another word for guarding a player. One player marks another by following him around the field, preventing him from taking the ball towards the net, making an easy pass or getting the ball from a teammate. The defensive player uses his body position to block his opponent from moving forward towards the goal, usually trying to force him towards the sides of the field where the chance of scoring is much lower. Players forced to the sideline are effectively *cut off* from advancing further down the field.

Tackling
In soccer, tackling is the act of taking the ball away from a player by kicking or stopping it with one's feet. Tackling in American football conjures up images of one player driving another into the ground with a vicious hit to the body. In soccer, however, the tackler cannot pursue another player physically, but instead must go primarily after the ball. Only a minimal amount of shoulder-to-shoulder contact, called a *shoulder charge*, is permitted to knock the dribbler off balance. (See **Figure 15**) However, as long as the tackler hits the ball first, he will not be charged with a foul even if he knocks down his opponent. Tackling can often be risky because a defender may become off-balance after missing a tackle, allowing the

Figure 15: Shoulder charge.

attacker to proceed unmarked. The following tackling techniques are used:

- *Front Tackle*: A defender attempts to kick the ball away from an attacker by approaching him from a head-on position. (See **Figure 16**) Since the players are moving towards each other, timing is essential. If a tackler misses the ball but makes contact with the attacker, a foul is usually called.

- *Side Tackle*: When 2 opposing players are running in the same direction, it is harder for the defender to knock the ball completely from the attacker's control. In a side tackle, the defender tries to redirect the ball slightly with his foot in the hope that the attacker will overrun it.

- *Back Tackle*: A defender who is running behind an attacker attempts a tackle by swinging his leg in front of the ball. The defender may receive a foul if he trips the attacker and the *referee* determines that the defender was not in position to take the ball away. (See **Figure 17**)

Figure 16: Front tackle.

Figure 17: Back tackle.

- *Sliding Tackle*: The defender tries to take the ball away by sliding on the ground, feet first into the ball. Although this is the most exciting type of tackle, it is also the riskiest. If the tackler fails to dislodge the ball, he is on the ground and unable to halt the attacker's advance. For this reason, the sliding tackle is generally used only as a last resort. A sliding tackle may not be attempted from behind the attacker and must be directed solely at the ball; otherwise, the tackler may be penalized by a *direct free kick* and a *yellow card*, both of which are discussed in the chapter entitled **FOULS**. (See **Figure 18**)

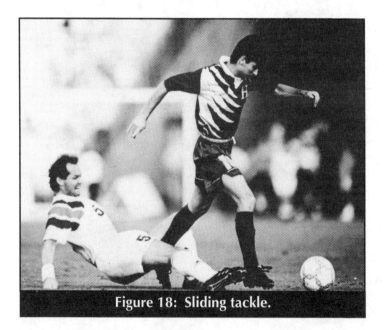

Figure 18: Sliding tackle.

In the next chapter entitled **PLAYER POSITIONS**, the different roles assigned to players on the same team are explained.

PLAYER POSITIONS

Soccer teams assign players to positions on the *field* where their individual skills can best be utilized. There are 4 general types of players: *forwards, midfielders* (or *halfbacks*), *defensemen* (or *fullbacks*) and *goalkeepers*. Each must perform different tasks. However, since the action in soccer flows freely between *offense* and *defense*, it will often occur during a game that *offensive players* need to play defense and *defenders* need to go on the attack. All players have the freedom to roam the field, going where the action is.

FORMATIONS

The rules of soccer allow 11 players per team on the field at one time, including 1 *goalie*. That leaves 10 players to divide among defensive, midfield and forward positions. Most teams use at least 3 defenders, 2 midfielders and 1 forward. The remaining 4 players are distributed in different ways, chosen by the coach in selecting a particular style of play for his team. The arrangements of the 10 players are called *formations*, denoted by listing the number of players at each position (excluding the goalie since there is always 1). For example:

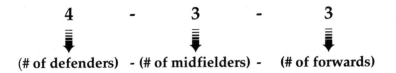

4 - **3** - **3**

(# of defenders)   - (# of midfielders) -   (# of forwards)

This formation is referred to as the *4-3-3*, and it is one of the more popular ones used in both professional and youth league soccer. **Figure 19** shows an example of where each player is positioned in the 4-3-3 while his team is on offense or defense, for both *man-to-man* and *zone* defenses (discussed later in this chapter). Two other popular formations are the *4-4-2* and the *4-2-4*.

KEY: L = Left   W = Wing   FB = Fullback
R = Right   M = Midfielder   CD = Central Defender

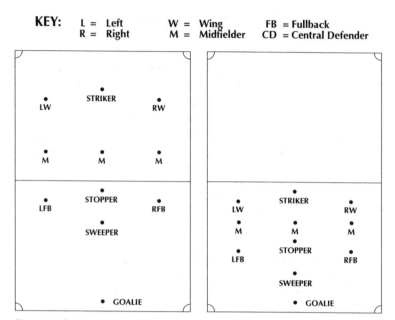

Team on offense, playing man-to-man   Team on defense, playing man-to-man

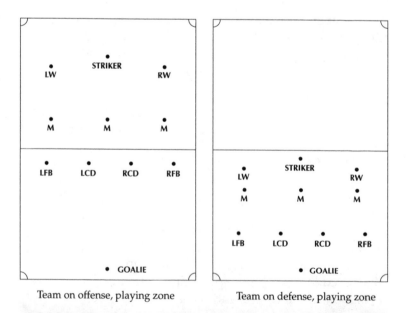

Team on offense, playing zone   Team on defense, playing zone

Figure 19: Player positions for the 4-3-3.

FORWARDS

Forwards are responsible for most of a team's scoring, so they usually play at the front of the offense where they can take most of the *shots*. Their ability to *score* usually determines the outcome of a game. They must possess great speed to get past defenders and the stamina to maintain an advantage throughout the game. Forwards also need to be agile *dribblers* to get around defenders and must have a strong and accurate shot from either foot to score *goals*. Finally, they need to be able to quickly analyze a *scoring opportunity* and take quick action.

There are 2 main types of forwards: *strikers* and *wingers*. A *forward line* consists of 1 or 2 strikers and 2 wingers who work together to try to score goals.

Strikers — They play towards the middle of the field, so they are in front of the opposition's goal more often and have greater opportunities to shoot. As the top goal *scorers* on the field, they are usually *marked* more closely and by the opposition's best defensive player, requiring them to play well under tight *defensive pressure*. They are the most powerful of the forwards because they need to take hard shots at the goal, both with their feet and their heads.

Wingers — These are the outside forwards, playing to the sides or *wings* of the strikers. Although they sometimes score, the wingers' job is to make accurate *passes* toward the middle of the field (called *crossing passes* or *crosses*) to the strikers to set up *scoring opportunities*. Wingers must be able to spot the open strikers and deliver passes with accuracy and timing. Since wingers are also responsible for advancing the ball deep into the opponent's end of the field, they are often the fastest players, the best dribblers and the best able to *beat* their defenders.

MIDFIELDERS

Midfielders play *behind* their team's forwards (closer to their own goal) and in front of their team's defenders.

Since they are responsible for linking together the offensive and defensive functions of a team, they are sometimes called *linkmen*. They are more commonly known as halfbacks because they have a split role: to provide the offense with good passes, initiating their team's attack when it has the ball, and to halt the opposition's attack before it gains momentum towards their own goal. When the opportunity arises, midfielders may participate in an attack on the opposition's goal, but they must remain prepared to help the defenders in their own half of the field.

Since they play both offense and defense, the midfielders are generally the most versatile players on a team. They run more than any other player, often more than 10 miles in one game, requiring them to have the stamina of long distance runners. Most teams play with either 2, 3 or 4 midfielders.

Midfielders are further specialized into *Attacking*, *Defending* and *Two-Way Midfielders*. These are not always rigid positions; depending on the circumstances, midfielders may switch during the game.

DEFENDERS
The role of the defenders (also called fullbacks) is to prevent the opposition from getting a good scoring opportunity. Taking the ball away from the attacking players is their primary goal, although just slowing the opposition's progress allows the defenders' teammates time to help repel the attack. A defender must be a master at *tackling* and have good speed to keep up with very quick opposing forwards. Finally, good defenders must also be able to anticipate the play of the opposing offensive players, positioning themselves well to challenge the attack.

Defenders are further specialized into 4 different positions: fullback, *central defender*, *stopper* and *sweeper*.

Fullbacks — They specialize in guarding the areas to the left and right sides of the goal and usually defend against the opposing team's wingers who try to advance the ball up the sides of the field. There are always 2 fullbacks on each team.

Central Defenders — In a zone defense (discussed below), these defenders are responsible for the center of the field, directly in front of their own goal. They have the critical task of warding off any attacking player who comes near the front of the goal, so their physical play and tackling are more important than their speed. In a man-to-man defense (discussed below), this position does not exist.

Stopper — In a man-to-man defense, one stopper and one sweeper play in place of two central defenders. The stopper is the defender that *marks* the best scorer on the attacking team, often the opposition's striker, so he must possess great concentration to avoid being *faked* out.

Sweeper — The job of this player fits his name — he is responsible for cleaning and clearing away the balls that have gotten away from the other defenders. He is a team's last line of defense in front of the goalkeeper.

Defenses
Typically, a team plays with 4 defenders. The way they are utilized depends on which of the 2 main types of defenses a team adopts: man-to-man or zone. The positioning of the players in each of these defenses was shown earlier in **Figure 19**.

Man-to-Man — In this type of defense, 3 of the 4 defenders each mark a different forward from the other team. Each defender follows his assigned forward wherever he goes,

37

thwarting his attempts to score. The fourth defender, the sweeper, roams the field, assisting his 3 teammates where needed. This is the most common type of defense for national-level teams.

Zone — This defense assigns each defender to a particular area in front of or around his team's goal in which he is responsible for marking any attacker that enters. The zone is often used in youth league games but rarely in professional competition. Norway is the biggest exception, relying heavily on the zone defense. The only other top *national team* to occasionally use a zone defense is the Swiss team.

GOALKEEPER
Perhaps the player having the greatest impact on the outcome of the game is the goalkeeper or *goalie*. His job is to prevent any shots from getting into the *net* behind him. Because of the difficulty of this task, he is allowed to use his arms and hands. Goalies take advantage of this privilege by catching the ball when they can, or by just tipping a shot headed for the net with their hands to deflect it over or around the goal. Sometimes, the goalie quickly moves out in front of the goal to snatch the ball before a player can shoot it, or jumps high into the air to grab a pass near the goal. However, the goalie is only allowed to use his hands within the *penalty area* or he is called for a *foul*.

Another important task for the goalkeeper is distributing the ball to his teammates. Because the goalie ends up with the ball so often, he must be adept at starting his team's attack. Depending on the situation, goalies either roll, throw or kick the ball to their teammates. The quality of these passes, called *outlet passes*, often determines the success of his team's attack.

Goalies must have talents that are required of no other players on the field. They must have excellent hand-eye coordination and quick reflexes to respond to shots that can exceed 80 miles per hour and are often taken from close range. Since a single person cannot protect all 24 feet of a goal's width at one time, goalies must also have excellent judgment and anticipation to position themselves in the right area in front of the net to prepare for a shot. They must be agile and able to dive in any direction to get a ball, including towards the ground. (See **Figure 20**) Finally, they must be fearless and tough, able to face blistering shots at their head and willing to throw their bodies into the air or down at the ground to snare loose balls.

Figure 20: Diving goalie.

All players, whatever their position, must obey the rules of soccer or risk being penalized. The next 3 chapters, on **THE OFFICIALS**, the **OFFSIDE RULE** and **FOULS** describe these rules and the people who enforce them.

THE OFFICIALS

The general conduct of a soccer game is controlled by 3 *officials:* 1 *referee* and 2 *linesmen.* These officials work together to stop and restart play, keep track of the score and the time remaining, and cite violations of the rules. Rule violations are called *fouls* for which the referees assess *free kicks.* In collegiate play, there is a separate *timekeeper* and *scorekeeper.*

The officials use different gestures to signal their decisions so that both the teams and the spectators understand what is happening on the *field.* These are illustrated in the **OFFICIALS' HAND SIGNALS** section. Officials wear uniforms that distinguish them from the players on either team. Since the officials are considered part of the field, if the ball hits one while he is standing *in bounds,* play continues uninterrupted.

THE REFEREE
The referee is the chief official and his decisions are final. He acts as the timekeeper, carrying the *official game clock* with him so he can signal when each *period* is over. He can decide to extend the length of any period beyond the point that his clock has expired to make up for time spent attending to injured players or time wasted by a team that is stalling. This is called *injury time.*

The referee is the only person on the field who has the authority to stop play, and he does so by blowing his whistle. It is his responsibility to stop play whenever a rule has been violated or a player is seriously injured. However, it is also the referee's duty to use his discretion to refrain from calling a foul that would give the offending team an advantage by stopping play. This is called the *Advantage Rule,* discussed in the chapter on **FOULS**.

The referee also has the sole power to suspend any player he believes is displaying dangerous or unsportsmanlike behavior. He disciplines such players by using a solid-colored *yellow card* or *red card*. Because soccer is an international game, these simple colors are used to avoid any potential confusion caused by language differences. The referee holds one of these playing card-sized cards above his head for the offending player and spectators to see. (See **Figure 21**)

Figure 21: Referee holding yellow card or red card.

A yellow card is used to warn a player that his conduct is unacceptable and that he will be ejected upon his next serious offense. A red card signifies that a player must leave the field for the remainder of the game, and is given either for a second violation (two yellow cards are equivalent to a red card), or for a more serious infraction such as intentionally injuring another player. This player's team must play the rest of the game *shorthanded*. In college, a player receiving a red card is also suspended for his team's next game.

THE LINESMEN
The linesmen's sole duty is to assist the referee in making his decisions. Primarily, linesmen monitor the *sidelines* and

goal lines to determine when and where a ball goes *out of bounds*. Each linesman is responsible for monitoring one sideline and one goal line and carries a *flag* to signal to the referee whether there should be a *throw-in*, *goal kick* or *corner kick*, and which team will take it. When the ball goes out of bounds, the nearest linesman points his flag at the goal of the team that last touched it. The referee usually takes the linesman's advice but makes the final ruling himself, accompanied by his own hand signal. Linesmen also signal to the referee when they see a rule violation or a seriously injured player that the referee has not noticed.

Now that we have met the officials, it is time to discuss the rules that keep them the busiest — **THE OFFSIDE RULE** and **FOULS**.

THE OFFSIDE RULE

This is probably the most misunderstood of all the rules of soccer because it involves the action of several players at one time. The offside rule exists to prevent offensive players from waiting for a pass near the opposition's goal where they could easily *score*. When the *referee* whistles an *offside* violation against a team, he stops play and awards the non-offending team an *indirect free kick*.

The rule states that no *offensive player* may receive a *forward pass* when he is in an *offside position* if doing so gives him an advantage. An offside position means that there are fewer than 2 opposing *defensive players* (usually the *goalie* and 1 other *defender*) between a player and the *goal* he is attacking. A player is not offside if he is exactly even with 1 or both of these defensive players. **Figure 22** shows that player A2 is in an offside position because only the goalie B3 is between him and the goal. **Figure 23** shows that player A2 is *on-side* (opposite of offside) because 2 defensive players, B2 and goalie B3, are between him and the goal.

One important condition to this rule is that the position of the player receiving a pass is relevant only at the instant the ball left his teammate's foot. This means that as long as a *receiver* started on-side, even if he runs into an offside position while the ball is traveling from the passer to him, he is not considered offside. In the example shown in **Figure 24**, when the ball was passed, player A2 had defensive player B1 and goalie B3 between him and the goal, making him on-side.

Likewise, a player that starts offside when the pass is kicked to him is called for the violation even if he ends up on-side when he receives the pass. **Figure 25** shows that A2 was offside when the ball left the foot of teammate A1.

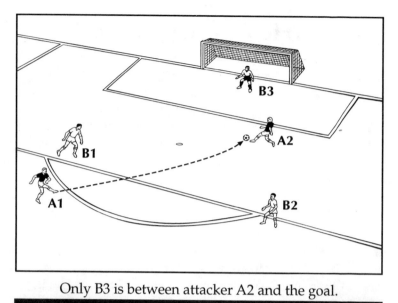

Only B3 is between attacker A2 and the goal.

Figure 22: Offside.

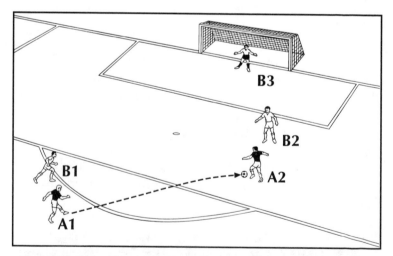

Two defenders, B2 and goalie B3, are between A2 and the goal.

Figure 23: On-side.

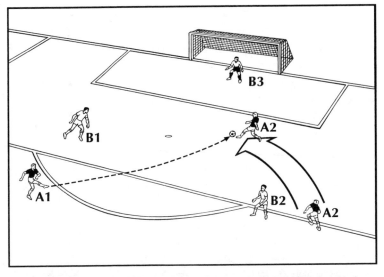

B1 and goalie B3 were between A2 and the goal when ball left A1's foot.

Figure 24: On-side.

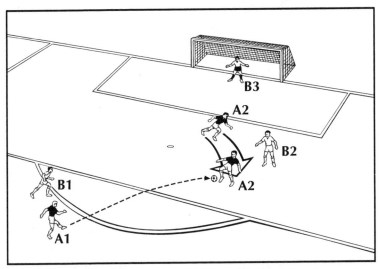

Only goalie B3 was between A2 and the goal when ball left A1's foot.

Figure 25: Offside.

Other important conditions to this rule are:

- Offside should not be called unless a player has gained an advantage by being in such a position.

- Offside is not called against a receiver who was in his own defensive half of the field when the ball left his teammate's foot.

- Offside is not called when a player receives the ball in an offside position directly from a *throw-in, goal kick* or *corner kick*.

- A player in an offside position can be cited if he obstructs an opposing defensive player or goalie in any way (including blocking his vision), even if he never receives the ball.

FOULS

A *foul* is an individual violation of the rules of soccer. Whenever a player commits a foul, the *referee* stops play and orders it restarted by an *indirect free kick*, a *direct free kick* or a *penalty kick* depending on the severity of the violation. All of these methods of restarting the game were discussed in the chapter **HOW THE GAME IS PLAYED**.

INDIRECT FREE KICK

An indirect free kick is awarded for less serious infractions. A *goal* cannot be scored directly from an indirect kick but must first touch another player. The kick is taken at the spot on the *field* where the foul occurred. The following fouls call for an indirect free kick:

- *Dangerous Play*: when a player attempts a play that the referee considers dangerous (even if it is only dangerous to that player); for example, trying to kick the ball out of the *goalie*'s hands, whether or not contact is made.

- *Charging* Player Without the Ball: using a *shoulder charge* against a player who is not close enough to the ball to play it.

- Charging the Goalkeeper: illegal only against a goalie in his *goal area* who is not holding the ball. In collegiate rules, charging the goalie is illegal only when he is inside his *penalty area* and holding the ball.

- Intentional *Obstruction*: when a player, instead of going after the ball, uses his body to obstruct another player from playing it.

- Backward *Pass* Handled by the Goalie: when a goalie uses his hands on a ball kicked to him by a teammate; rule encourages teams to play the ball forward to speed up the game.

- *Carrying the Ball*: when a goalkeeper takes more than 4 steps while holding or bouncing the ball; to avoid a foul, he must release the ball before taking his fifth step and not touch it again until another player has.

- 5-Second Limit for Goalie (college rule only): when a goalkeeper holds the ball for more than 5 seconds.

INDIRECT FREE KICK WITH YELLOW CARD

The following fouls call for disciplinary action against a player, earning him a *yellow card* in addition to giving the opposition an indirect free kick:

- Dissension: when a player argues with *officials* verbally or through gestures.

- Persistent Rule Breaking: when a player continually breaks the rules of soccer.

- Unsportsmanlike Conduct: when a player displays rude manners on the field.

- Entering/Leaving Without Permission: when a player leaves or re-enters the field without permission from the referee.

INDIRECT FREE KICK WITH RED CARD

Severe personal infractions call for further disciplinary action. In addition to an indirect free kick awarded to the opposing team, the offending player receives a *red card*, removing him from the rest of the game. His team may not use a *substitute* to replace him. These offenses are:

- Violent play
- Use of foul or abusive language
- Serious foul play (for example, impeding an obvious scoring attempt by intentionally fouling an opponent or handling the ball)
- Continued misconduct after receiving a yellow card

DIRECT FREE KICK OR PENALTY KICK

Some fouls are more serious than those calling for an indirect kick, and for these, the non-offending team is awarded a direct free kick. A team may score on a direct kick without the ball first touching another player. If any of these fouls are committed by the defense in its own penalty area, the referee awards a *penalty kick* to the opposing *offense* because an infraction near the goal is assumed to have hindered a *scoring opportunity*. These fouls include:

- Touching the ball with the hands or arms, called a *hand ball* (Exceptions: a goalie within his penalty area or any player when the ball unintentionally hits his hand or arm)
- Kicking or striking an opponent
- Tripping an opponent
- Jumping into an opponent
- Spitting on an opponent
- *Charging* violently or from behind
- *Holding* (See **Figure 26**) or pushing an opponent

Figure 26: Holding.

THE ADVANTAGE RULE

The *Advantage Rule* exists to make sure that a foul does not provide an advantage to the team that committed the offense. It is the referee's duty to use his judgment and decide not to stop play if the fouled team is able to maintain *possession* and continue to play despite the foul. For example, if a *forward* on Team A is tripped by a *midfielder* from Team B but gets off a good pass to a teammate before he falls down, the referee should not call a foul because it would give Team B an advantage by stopping Team A's momentum. The referee allows the teams to *play on*. At the next stoppage of play, the referee may still give a yellow or red card to an individual who committed a serious offense.

The section entitled **OFFICIALS' HAND SIGNALS,** which shows the signals officials use to communicate to each other, the players and the spectators, can be found at the end of this book.

THINGS TO LOOK FOR DURING PLAY / STRATEGY

A soccer game consists of a great deal of back and forth action between 2 teams. Players seem to run after the ball without much organization. However, a simple review of the strategy that teams use to try to win soccer games will help you understand the purpose of player movements and tactics.

ATTACK STRATEGIES
For a team to advance the ball towards the opponent's end of the *field* and *score*, its players follow some basic principles about *offensive* or *attack* strategy.

Creating Space
How players move without the ball is just as important as what they do when they have it. A player moving without the ball is dangerous because a well-placed *pass* from a teammate can give him the ball undefended and with a running start. Because this moving player is a threat, he draws *defenders* away from the *ball carrier*, *creating space* for his teammates by freeing them of some defenders.

One example of creating space is called the *overlap*. This is where a *winger* moves away from the *sideline* towards the center of the field to draw defenders with him, creating space for his teammate to advance the ball undefended along the edge of the field towards the opposition's goal.

Breaks and Advantages
In soccer, numerical superiority is important. A team that temporarily has more players than the opposition in an area will usually have an *open* man, or one that is not *marked*, who can take shots or pass the ball while undefended. One of the objectives of an offense is to try to create these *advantages* by quickly advancing many of its

players towards the opposition's goal before all of the opposing players have had a chance to retreat and defend. These quick runs are called *breaks*. For example, an offense that threatens with 3 forwards defended by 2 opposing players (not including the *goalie*) is on a *3-on-2 break*, or a *3-on-2 advantage*. There are also *2-on-1 breaks*, *3-on-1 breaks* or any other combination of offensive and defensive players.

The extreme example of the break is the *breakaway*, where an attacker with the ball approaches the goal undefended. This exciting play pits a sole *attacker* against the *goaltender* in a one-on-one showdown.

Passing
The quickest and easiest way for a team to advance the ball towards the opponent's goal is by passing. Therefore, passing is an integral part of effective offensive play.

Long vs. Short Passes — There are advantages and drawbacks of both long and short passes. Generally, a series of short passes allows a team to advance the ball with less chance of losing *possession*. A properly placed long pass, however, can replace a number of short passes by quickly getting the ball to a teammate much closer to the opposing goal, skipping over several defenders in one big step. Although the long pass can be an exciting play, several factors work against its completion. Long passes stay in the air a long time, allowing defensive players time to position themselves to intercept the pass. Also, a strong wind may hamper the accuracy of a long pass.

Types of Passes — Teams use the following types of passes to move the ball effectively against the defense:

- *Lead Pass*: A pass sent ahead of a moving teammate to arrive at a location at the same time he does.

- *Crossing Pass* (or *Cross*): A pass sent across the field, from one side of the field towards the middle or opposite side; the best way for attacking players to get the ball to *open* teammates who are in a better position to shoot at the goal.

- *Through Pass*: A pass sent to a teammate to get him the ball *behind* his defender; used by the attacking team to *penetrate* a line of defenders without having to *dribble* through them; often gives the attacking team a numerical advantage close to the goal.

- *Square Pass*: A pass to a teammate alongside the *ball carrier* running in the same direction. This is often used to get the ball to a player who is in a better position to penetrate the defense.

- *Wall Pass*: Allows the ball carrier to get past his defender without having to dribble by him. The ball carrier sends the ball to a teammate, then runs behind his own defender and quickly receives a pass back. It is called a wall pass because the ball carrier's teammate returns the ball much like a wall would. This is the same as the "give-and-go" in basketball.

Shielding
Teams try to maintain possession of the ball because this allows them to control and maneuver it into a position to score while keeping it away from the opposing team's offense. An important way players prevent nearby opponents from taking the ball away is by *shielding*. Also called *screening*, shielding is when a ball carrier keeps his body between the ball and a defender closely marking him. The defender will have a difficult time successfully *tackling* and removing the ball from such a player without committing a *foul*. Players try to shield the ball until the defender backs off or a teammate arrives to receive a pass.

Fakes
One of the most entertaining skills to watch in soccer, *fakes* or *feints* are an art used by the ball carrier to make a

defender think the ball carrier is going to move, pass or shoot in a certain direction when he is not. Since defenders try to follow most movements made by the offensive player they are marking, fakes are often an effective method for the attacker to get free. Body control and ball control are the keys to successful faking. A player's chest usually gives his true intentions away and a good defender watches this and ignores extraneous movement. The world's great ball handlers all have a repertoire of effective fakes.

<u>Corner Kick Strategy</u>
A *corner kick* is different from most of the other restart plays because it gives the attacking team a good chance of scoring. To enhance its chances, the attacking team places most of its players near the *goalmouth*. That way, when the kick is launched towards the front of the goal, the likelihood of an offensive player putting the ball into the *net* increases.

The kicker has a variety of options. He can:

- *Loft* a pass in front of the goal where teammates in the area try to jump and *head* the ball into the goal.
- Hit a *banana kick* that curves towards the goal. Such a shot could go directly into the net for a goal or be deflected past the goalkeeper by a teammate.
- Kick a hard shot to an area right in front of the net. It may be kicked or headed into the goal by a teammate or *deflected* in by accident off a defender.
- Kick a short pass to a teammate playing near the corner. This player may not be marked because he is not close to the goal.

DEFENSIVE STRATEGY
While it is the objective of the offensive team to maintain possession of the ball and advance it, the defense's mission is to take the ball away and halt the offense's advance. In general, defenders try to place their bodies between the

54

ball and the goal, preventing the attackers from moving the ball forward. Defenders also try to keep attacking players with the ball towards the sides of the field, where any shot at the goal needs to be taken from a sharper and more difficult angle.

Zone vs. Man-to-Man Defense

The type of defense a team chooses often depends on the skills of its defensive players. A *man-to-man* defense relies on each player to individually mark another player, but also uses a *sweeper* to mark any attacker that *beats* his defender. If a particular offensive player is far superior to the defender marking him, it is called a *mismatch*. That defender can expect little support from teammates who are busy marking their own attackers — the sweeper is the only player who might possibly assist a beaten defender. Most professional teams favor a man-to-man defense because it assigns concrete responsibility for each defender to mark an attacking player. At that level, the chances of a severe mismatch are lower since most players are highly skilled.

Zone defense, on the other hand, relies more on teamwork and coordination and less on the individual ability of the defenders. Since players cover an area instead of individuals, an offensive player who succeeds in getting by one defender may face another in the same area. This same teamwork, however, can also be the undoing of the zone defense, since players may have trouble deciding who is responsible for marking attackers playing in between the zones. Because there may be large differences in talent among young players, many youth league teams use the zone defense to spread defensive responsibility among several players.

Counterattack

Besides stopping the opposing team from scoring, another main goal of the defenders is to start their own team's attack towards the opposing team's goal. As soon as a team regains possession of the ball, defensive players become offensive players, passing the ball to a *midfielder* or *forward*, or dribbling with it, sometimes all the way past the *midfield line*. This is called a *counterattack*, and it is the defender's duty to get it started.

GOALIE STRATEGIES
Ball Distribution
Since the *goalie* touches the ball so often during a soccer match, how he distributes the ball to teammates often determines the success or failure of a team's counterattacks. The goalie may either throw, roll, *drop kick* or kick the ball off of the ground. The goalie chooses how to distribute the ball depending on the location of opposing players. If they are close to the goal, the goalie will drop kick the ball over their heads and down the field to keep it away from them. On the other hand, if they are playing away from the goal, a long pass would probably be intercepted, so the goalie will roll or kick the ball to a nearby teammate to begin the counterattack near to his goal.

Cutting Down the Angle
When an attacker dribbles the ball towards the goal, the goalie will often come out of the goal several feet to *cut down the angle* of the dribbler, leaving him less net to shoot at by making himself closer and larger to the shooter. However, this is risky because if an attacker were to get the ball past the goalie, he would have an open shot at the net.

YOUTH LEAGUE DIFFERENCES

Organized youth soccer is booming in the U.S. Of the many organizations that have been established to oversee and improve the competition and the fun, the 2 that boast the most members are the United States Youth Soccer Association (*USYSA*) and the American Youth Soccer Organization (*AYSO*). Both organize and administer youth league games and provide information and equipment to *referees*, coaches and players.

USYSA is the nation's largest youth soccer organization with nearly 2 million registered members. It is the Youth Division of the *USSF*, the *FIFA*-endorsed governing body of soccer in the U.S. AYSO is another organization with over 430,000 members nationwide. Although both generally follow FIFA's *Laws of the Game*, they have devised special rules and guidelines for children of all ages who play soccer. This chapter outlines the most important areas where the guidelines followed by youth leagues depart from the Laws.

USYSA and AYSO organize children into divisions by age, as shown in **Tables 3** and **4** respectively. Several rules depend on the age of the children, and are explained below.

LENGTH OF GAME
One of the major differences between adult and youth play is the length of the game. Younger children tend to have lower stamina than adults, so both organizations have shortened their games in accordance with the age of the players. For children in the Under-10 division, USYSA has also divided the game into 4 quarters instead of 2 *halves*. The maximum allowable lengths of each half are listed by division in **Tables 3** and **4**.

TABLE 3: USYSA YOUTH RULES BY AGE

AGE (YEARS)	LENGTH OF EACH HALF	FIELD SIZE (YARDS)	GOAL SIZE (FEET) (HEIGHT x WIDTH)	# OF PLAYERS
Under 19	45 minutes	FIFA	8 x 24	11
Under 17	45 minutes	FIFA	8 x 24	11
Under 16	40 minutes	FIFA	8 x 24	11
Under 14	35 minutes	FIFA	8 x 24	11
Under 12	30 minutes	FIFA	8 x 24	11
Under 10	25 minutes	50 x 80	7 x 21	9
Under 8	24 minutes*	30 x 50	6 x 12	4
Under 6	16 minutes*	20 x 25	4 x 6	3

* Divided into 4 quarters

TABLE 4: AYSO YOUTH RULES BY AGE

AGE (YEARS)	DIVISION #	LENGTH OF EACH HALF	BALL DIAMETER (INCHES)**	BALL WEIGHT (OUNCES)**
Under 19	1	45 minutes	26.5 - 28.0	14 - 16
Under 16	2	40 minutes	26.5 - 28.0	14 - 16
Under 14	3	35 minutes	26.5 - 28.0	14 - 16
Under 12	4	30 minutes	25.0 - 26.5	12 - 14
Under 10	5	25 minutes	25.0 - 26.5	12 - 14
Under 8	6	20 minutes	23.0 - 25.0	10 - 12
Under 6	7	20 minutes	23.0 - 25.0	10 - 12

** Also applies to USYSA

SIZE OF BALL
Youth soccer officials believe that smaller children should play with a smaller ball so they can more easily kick, *dribble* or *head* it. The ball sizes used in the games of younger children are listed in **Table 4**. Since the guidelines for both organizations are identical, they are shown only

once in the AYSO table. Starting with the Under-14 division, older players use the same standard-sized ball as in international play.

FIELD AND GOAL SIZE

USYSA recommends that children under 10 play on smaller *fields* of the sizes shown in **Table 3**. On these fields, the other markings are also smaller. On the other hand, AYSO allows youth teams to play on fields of whatever dimensions are agreed upon by the officials in a given region. Goal size, field length and width, and other markings may differ from the official FIFA requirements. One exception to this is during AYSO post-season or *playoff* games, when the field must adhere strictly to FIFA requirements (i.e., must be at least 100 yards long by 50 yards wide).

NUMBER OF PLAYERS

Both organizations recommend that teams with young children play with fewer than 11 players per side (called *small-sided games*) so that each child gets to participate more and develop his or her skills faster. To encourage participation, even players that do not start in a game must play at least half of the game, assuring that no player will be relegated just to bench-warming. USYSA gives specific guidelines for the number of players in its Under-10 age groups, as shown in **Table 3**. In these games a *goalie* is optional, and if a team chooses to use one, players are encouraged to take turns playing the position.

SUBSTITUTIONS

Each league recommends that *substitutions* be made midway through each half (or after each quarter when 4 *periods* are played) and at *halftime* to assure that playing time is split evenly among all players. In AYSO, the referee makes sure that all children participate by stopping the game halfway through each period to account on his lineup card for which players are in the game.

EQUIPMENT

Both organizations require that all players wear protective *shinguards* on each leg. Players are also allowed to wear soft rubber *cleats* for shoes. Neither organization allows players to wear anything that might be dangerous to other players. AYSO rules specifically forbid youngsters to play when they are wearing a cast or splint to avoid the risk of injury.

COACHES

The participation of coaches in a soccer game is to be kept to a minimum according to the rules. In AYSO, a maximum of 2 coaches may be present from each team and neither may leave the *coaches' area*. This is an area along the *sideline* extending 10 yards to either side of the *center line*.

GOALIE PROTECTION

AYSO rules extend the protection that FIFA's Laws gives to goalies. According to FIFA rules, attacking players may only legally *charge* a goalie if he ventures outside his *goal area*. Similar to the collegiate rules, AYSO protects the goalie from being charged anywhere within the *penalty area*, a much larger area of protection (44 x 18 yards for AYSO vs. 20 x 6 yards for FIFA).

OTHER RULES

While AYSO conforms closely to FIFA on most of its other guidelines, USYSA has altered the rules for the youngest children to make the game even simpler for them. Some of these are:

- All *free kicks* are *indirect* (Under-8)
- No *penalty kicks* are awarded (Under-8)
- *Corner kicks* are replaced by *throw-ins* (Under-6)

By following these guidelines, youth leagues will get the maximum possible enjoyment out of friendly soccer competition.

ROAD TO THE
WORLD CUP TOURNAMENT

The *World Cup* is an international soccer competition held every 4 years between the top professional teams in the world, pitting nation against nation. The tournament is the most watched event in the world by far — 3 BILLION people, over half of the world's population, watched the 1990 World Cup, with the final game alone attracting a television audience of nearly 1.5 BILLION. Its games evoke strong feelings of national pride among competing countries and a *qualifying match* once even led to armed conflict.

The road to the tournament spans 2 long years and consists of the *Qualifying Draw*, the *Qualifying Tournament*, and *The Draw*. Then, 24 teams play in the 5-*round*, 52-game World Cup tournament. The team that survives all this to win the World Cup has truly earned its title.

QUALIFYING DRAW & TOURNAMENT

Any of *FIFA*'s 178 member countries may enter the Qualifying Tournament by paying an entry fee. Two years before The Draw, qualifying begins with the Qualifying Draw, a random division of teams into regional groups. These groups then play *matches* amongst themselves to earn the right to play in the World Cup tournament. In 1994, a record 141 teams participated in qualifying, playing a total of over 500 matches.

Each team plays every other team in its regional group twice, and the teams with the best records qualify for the World Cup. FIFA pre-determines how many teams from each region deserve to qualify for the tournament based on the quality of that region's teams. Then, that number of top teams (based on their *win-draw-loss* record, explained below in **THE TOURNAMENT**) is invited to The Draw, where teams are randomly grouped for the World Cup. A total of only 22 teams will qualify, in addition to the 2 automatic entrants — the champion of the previous World Cup and the current tournament host.

In qualifying for the 1994 World Cup, for example, 32 European teams were split into 7 groups. FIFA determined that the best 13 of these teams should qualify for the tournament because there are so many good soccer teams in Europe. Other regions represented with fewer teams are Asia (2 teams in 1994), Africa (3), *CONCACAF* (2 or 3 including host U.S.), South America (3 or 4) and Oceania (a maximum of 1). In 1994, the 1990 World Cup champion West Germany and the host United States were automatically entered into the tournament.

THE DRAW
The Draw attracts an enormous television audience of more than 500 million people without a single soccer ball being kicked. It is an entertainment extravaganza centered around determining the matchups, or the "who plays whom", among the 24 teams who qualified for the tournament. Under the current system, small ping pong-sized colored balls, each representing a team, are picked out of 4 fishbowls and divided into 6 groups. These determine which teams will play one another in the initial stage of games called the first round.

To distribute the strongest teams evenly across all groups, each of the bowls is filled with 6 teams of similar strength. One bowl at a time is emptied of all its balls one-by-one, and the balls are placed randomly in one of the 6 groups (Groups A through F), assuring that similarly-ranked teams do not end up in the same group. For example, in the 1994 Draw, the top teams of Argentina, Belgium, Brazil, Germany, Italy and the U.S. were placed together in one bowl so that each of these teams would be placed in a separate group. (The U.S. was included in this bowl as the host).

The process is not completely random, though. When The Draw would place 2 teams from the same qualifying region in a group together, officials intervene to place one into another group. This prevents the same matches played in qualifying from being repeated early in the tournament. The exception to this rule is Europe's 13 teams, which because of their great number must be placed 2 or 3 to a group. In this case, officials make sure that no group draws all 4 of its teams from Europe.

The Draw is critical to a team's success because it determines the first round opponents it must defeat to advance to the second round, called the *Round of 16*. Despite measures to keep the strength of the groups even, however, luck sometimes does put together 4 great teams in a single group. In the 1986 World Cup, teams from West Germany, Denmark, Uruguay and Scotland were placed together in a group later termed the "Group of Death" because they were all such powerful teams. This happened again in the 1994 Draw, as 4 of the top 10 teams in the world, Italy, Ireland, Mexico and Norway ended up in the same group.

THE TOURNAMENT

The World Cup tournament format starting with the second round is illustrated in **Figure 28**. In the first round, each of the 24 teams plays the other 3 teams in its group once. Teams advance to the Round of 16 based on their win-draw-loss record for those 3 games. The teams are compared on the basis of *points*, calculated as follows:

- 3 points for each game won (NEW for World Cup 1994)
- 1 point for each game that ends in a *draw*
- 0 points for each game lost

If teams have the same number of points, the team with the larger goal differential (*goals* scored minus goals by the opposition) in group play advances. The 16 teams that make it to the second round include the top 2 from each group, and the top 4 overall third place teams.

Until the 1994 World Cup, only 2 points were awarded for each win. In this system, teams were content to play for a draw since they would each receive half of the value of a win. To promote more aggressive play and more offense, FIFA decided to award an extra point for a win. This change was not implemented in time to apply to the qualifying matches for the 1994 World Cup.

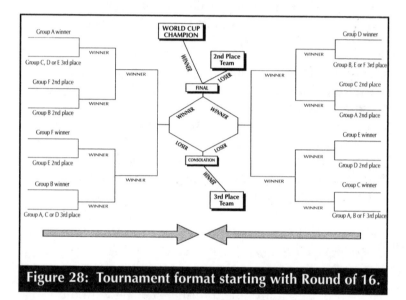

Figure 28: Tournament format starting with Round of 16.

Starting with the Round of 16, all games are *single elimination* (a single defeat eliminates a team from the tournament). Since there must be a winner in each game, there can be no draws. Teams still tied after *regulation* play two 15-minute *overtime* periods, and, if they remain tied after that, the game is decided by a *tiebreaker* of *penalty shots*. After the Round of 16, only 8 teams remain to play in the third round, the *quarterfinals*. The 4 winners of the quarterfinal matches advance to the fourth round, or the *semifinals*. The 2 losers of those matches play the *consolation match* for third place. One day later, the winners square off in the World Cup Final match to determine the champion and runner-up.

HISTORY OF THE WORLD CUP

Initially established as a competition for soccer players who turned professional and were therefore no longer eligible to play in the Olympics (then an amateur-only event), the first *World Cup* tournament was played in 1930. Since then, it has grown to become the world's largest single-sport event, watched by over half of its population. A list of World Cup champions is shown in **Table 5**.

The winners of the early World Cup tournaments were given a solid gold cup designed by French sculptor Abel Lafleur to hold for 4 years. This was named the *Jules Rimet Trophy* after the long-time President of *FIFA* who was responsible for arranging the first World Cup competition. The trophy, which was usually passed on to the next World Cup champion, was permanently awarded to Brazil in 1970 as the first nation to win 3 World Cup titles.

Over the years, despite great measures to protect the cup, some interesting things happened to it. First, during World War II, the cup was buried by an Italian soccer official to hide and protect it from occupying troops. Then, in 1966, the cup was stolen from the World Cup tournament in England while it was being protected by 6 security guards at a London stamp exhibition. Again, the cup was found buried, this time in a London suburb. Finally, in 1983, 13 years after the cup was permanently given to Brazil, it was stolen from a display box in Rio de Janeiro and never recovered.

After the Jules Rimet Trophy was awarded to Brazil, it was replaced by the *FIFA World Cup*, a solid gold statue designed by Italian sculptor Silvio Gazamiga. (See **Figure 29**) Today, this trophy is still given to the champion of each tournament to keep for the next 4 years.

TABLE 5: WORLD CUP CHAMPIONSHIP MATCHES

YEAR	VENUE	WINNER	RUNNER-UP	SCORE
1930	Montevideo, Uruguay	Uruguay	Argentina	4-2
1934	Rome, Italy	Italy	Czechoslovakia	2-1
1938	Paris, France	Italy	Hungary	4-2
1950	Rio de Janeiro, Brazil	Uruguay	Brazil	2-1
1954	Berne, Switzerland	West Germany	Hungary	3-2
1958	Stockholm, Sweden	Brazil	Sweden	5-2
1962	Santiago, Chile	Brazil	Czechoslovakia	3-1
1966	Wembley, England	England	West Germany	4-2
1970	Mexico City, Mexico	Brazil	Italy	4-1
1974	Munich, West Germany	West Germany	Holland	2-1
1978	Buenos Aires, Argentina	Argentina	Holland	3-1
1982	Madrid, Spain	Italy	West Germany	3-1
1986	Mexico City, Mexico	Argentina	West Germany	3-2
1990	Rome, Italy	West Germany	Argentina	1-0
1994	Pasadena, California			

Figure 29: The FIFA World Cup.

SUMMARY OF WORLD CUPS

1930: Reigning Olympic champion Uruguay lured the first World Cup to its shores by building a new stadium and paying for travel expenses of visiting teams. The government was insulted when many nations still refused to make the difficult ocean crossing, and those that did come suffered. The result: a championship game between 2 South American teams and a victory for the host.

The presence of the U.S. at this first World Cup tournament created one of the more humorous moments in World Cup history. During a game, the American trainer, while running to aid an injured player on the field, tripped and fell down, breaking a bottle of chloroform he was carrying. He fell unconscious and needed to be carried off the field while the player he was supposed to treat stayed in the game.

1934, 1938: Italy won both World Cups, first as the host and then in neighboring France.

1942, 1946: Canceled due to World War II.

1950: This World Cup featured the biggest upset in World Cup history, when the lowly U.S. team upset England, the most dominant team in soccer for the past two decades, 1-0. Ironically, this was England's first World Cup appearance ever, as it had boycotted FIFA since 1926 to protest FIFA's abandonment of amateur soccer.

1954: The West German team used trickery to help them take the 1954 cup. Against Hungary (the favorites in the tournament), the Germans purposely played several reserve players in an early-round game to trick the Hungarians into thinking that the Germans were not very good. After crushing the Germans 8-3, the Hungarians were lulled into complacency — when the two teams met again in the finals, the Germans returned to full strength and upset Hungary, 3-2.

1958, 1962: The 1958 tournament featured the debut of 17-year-old *Pelé*, who would become the most recognized sports celebrity in the world. He helped his Brazilian team win its first World Cup. France's Just Fontaine scored 13 goals in the tournament, a record that still stands today. In 1962, Chile was awarded the event only to have an earthquake cripple its infrastructure. Only through the pleading of its leaders was Chile allowed to remain the host. The Brazilians won again despite a pulled muscle that prevented Pelé from playing for most of the tournament.

1966: The Brazilian team, on its way to a third straight World Cup, were upset by Portugal and its young star *Eusebio*, before even reaching the *quarterfinals*. In the first *overtime* World Cup final since 1934, England beat West Germany 4-2, as Geoff Hurst scored a *hat trick* (3 goals) for England, the first player ever to do so in a final game. For the first time, the World Cup was televised worldwide, exposing millions of Americans to the excitement of top-notch soccer, and contributing to the explosion of soccer's popularity in the U.S. in the 1970s.

1970: The Brazilians returned to win their third World Cup championship in 4 consecutive tournaments for which they were permanently awarded the Jules Rimet Trophy. Although Pelé was still at the peak of his career, his fourth straight World Cup appearance was to be his last. Prior to the tournament, a *qualifying match* in which El Salvador eliminated Honduras triggered 2 weeks of all-out war between the countries, later referred to as the "Football War."

1974: Because of improving defenses, the 1974 World Cup featured the lowest scoring games of any previous tournament. Amazingly, 2 of the 3 goals scored in the final game were on *penalty kicks*, a rarity in any game and the only ones ever awarded in a World Cup final. West Germany won its second title and was the first to take home the new FIFA World Cup.

1978: Argentina became the third host nation in 4 consecutive tournaments to win the World Cup. Even an Argentine group that had been attacking the government suspended its violence to allow the tournament to go on.

1982: *Paolo Rossi*'s return to soccer following a 2-year suspension for his alleged part in a bribery scandal was marked by a 3-game, 6-goal performance (including a *hat trick* against Brazil in the finals) that provided Italy with its third World Cup title. In the semifinal match, West Germany beat France in the first World Cup match decided by a *tiebreaker*.

1986: This World Cup was played in the heat, humidity and altitude of Mexico City. Argentine forward *Diego Maradona* single-handedly led his team to the World Cup title, scoring the only 2 goals in the semifinal victory over Belgium, and then *assisting* on the game-winning goal in the final against West Germany. He also scored what is possibly the most controversial goal in World Cup history. In the quarterfinal match against England, officials did not see Maradona propel a ball into the *net* with his hand and awarded Argentina the goal. Later, Maradona swore that it was "the hand of God" that came down and scored.

1990: The West Germans, now coached by former player *Franz Beckenbauer*, beat Argentina in a rematch of the previous tournament's final. The Argentines were disciplined a record number of times throughout the tournament, collecting 164 *yellow cards* and 16 *red cards*, and even had to finish the final game with only 9 players after 2 were ejected. Although the U.S. qualified for the first time since 1950, they lost all 3 of their World Cup matches against Czechoslovakia, Italy and Austria.

1994: The U.S. automatically qualified for this tournament as its host. The official mascot for the games is "Striker", a playful cartoon-character dog developed by Warner Brothers Animation Studios. Other details are provided in the chapter **WORLD CUP 1994.**

WORLD CUP 1994

VENUES

In 1994, the XV *World Cup* tournament is being played in the United States for the first time ever. Unlike most World Cups that are played within a single city or region, the 52 games are being played in and around 9 different cities across the U.S., spanning 3,000 miles and 3 time zones. Its *venues* are: Boston (Foxboro Stadium), Chicago (Soldier Field), Dallas (Cotton Bowl), Detroit (Pontiac Silverdome), Los Angeles (Rose Bowl, Pasadena), New York / New Jersey (Meadowlands, East Rutherford), Orlando (Citrus Bowl), San Francisco (Stanford Stadium, Palo Alto) and Washington, D.C. (RFK Stadium) — from June 17 through July 17.

Since *FIFA* requires that World Cup matches be played on grass, 2 stadiums are being converted from artificial turf: the Silverdome and the Meadowlands. Growing grass in the Silverdome will be an extra challenge because it is completely indoors! Special sod and intense solar lamps will be used to maintain the new surface.

RULE CHANGES

FIFA implemented some new rules to improve the excitement of the 1994 World Cup, including:

* Wins Worth 3 *points*: The value of a win in the first *round* standings has been increased from 2 points. This makes winning far more valuable than a *draw*, giving teams an incentive to play with a more offensive-minded style.

* Faking Injury: An automatic *yellow card* will be given to any player believed to be faking an injury. Only a player with a cut or serious injury may be treated on the field. Any player with a less serious injury must leave the field to receive medical attention and his

team must either replace him with a substitute or play *shorthanded* until he returns. FIFA had estimated that 80% of on-the-field injuries did not require immediate attention yet were taking an average of 4 minutes.

- Drug Testing: Two players from each team will be randomly selected and tested for drug use after each game.

- New Awards: Awards such as "the most entertaining" team will be given after the tournament.

WHO'S IN & WHO'S NOT

An unprecedented 9 out of 24 spots in the tournament were decided on the last day of qualifying, with many exciting matches going down to the wire. The following is a brief summary of teams who made it, and those who did not.

In:
- Bolivia: This tiny country of only 6.3 million citizens will play in its first World Cup since 1950.

- Greece: Qualifying for the first time ever, it is coached by a former U.S. *national team* coach.

- Nigeria: Has never played in a World Cup, despite winning FIFA's Under-17 World Championship twice (1985, 1993).

- Norway: Last qualified in 1938 when it lasted just one game.

- Saudi Arabia: Players were each awarded $100,000 and a Mercedes for qualifying.

- United States: Qualifies as World Cup host in only its second appearance since 1950.

- West Germany: Qualifies as 1990 World Cup champion.

Out:
- Denmark: This European champion failed to qualify, while its Scandinavian neighbors from Sweden and Norway did.

- England: Needed to win by 7 goals in the final qualifying match to make it, but won only by 6, beating San Marino, 7-1. The U.S., as host, was delighted that England, famous for its hooligan fans, missed qualifying for the first time since 1978 (especially surprising after its semifinal appearance in 1990).

- France: Needed only to tie Israel in the final qualifying match, but blew a 2-1 lead in the final minutes to lose 3-2. Will receive an automatic bid in 1998 as host.

- Zambia: Nearly qualified after a plane crash killed the entire team in April 1993. A completely new team needed only a tie to qualify but lost to Morocco 1-0.

WOMEN'S WORLD CHAMPIONSHIP

Women's soccer in the U.S. is no minor sport, as nearly 40% of America's 16 million soccer players are female. They have a great deal to be encouraged about with the victory of the U.S. women's *national team* in the inaugural *FIFA* Women's World Championship in 1991, the female equivalent of the *World Cup*. Like the World Cup, it is held every 4 years, with the next one scheduled for 1995 in Sweden.

The U.S. is hoping to lure the 1999 games by hosting the first-ever Chiquita Cup in 6 *venues*, immediately following the completion of the 1994 World Cup. This 4-team tournament hosted by the *USSF* involves the following teams: the U.S., 1991 runner-up Norway, European champion Germany and Asian champion China.

SOCCER IN THE U.S.

Amateur soccer is the fastest growing sport in the U.S., currently played by about 16 million Americans. Professional soccer, on the other hand, has never achieved nearly the popularity in the U.S. of other major sports such as football, baseball, basketball and hockey, which are all multi-billion dollar industries. Still, soccer in the U.S. has had a long and rich history.

EARLY U.S. SOCCER HISTORY

Native Indians were the first observed playing a kicking game on the continent, even before the Pilgrims arrived in the 1600s. Organized soccer was first played at the collegiate level, with the first game pitting Rutgers against Princeton in 1869. In 1873, they were joined by Yale and Columbia at a meeting to formally adopt the *English Football Association*'s Rules. Harvard, on the other hand, refused to attend and instead put its influential support behind *rugby* football, a sport which modified soccer to allow players to carry the ball with their hands. It took Harvard only 3 years to convince these other schools to adopt the Rugby Union rules.

The influence of Harvard was the most instrumental factor in making *American football* a much more popular collegiate sport than soccer in the U.S. Having chosen rugby over soccer, Harvard made further changes to rugby's rules during the next 5 years to establish American football as we know it today. Other schools followed suit, and soccer was relegated to becoming a minor sport in the U.S. for much of the next 100 years.

There *was* one successful U.S. professional soccer *league* started in the 1940s — the American Soccer League (*ASL*). It was composed of clubs with similar ethnic and social backgrounds (for example, the New York German Hungarians).

THE 1960s, 1970s AND THE NASL

Soccer was revived in the 1960s when sports entrepreneurs began to import talent from Europe and Latin America to form a professional league in the U.S. Professional soccer was booming overseas and organizers hoped to capitalize on the worldwide popularity of the game.

In 1960, sports promoter Bill Cox formed the International Soccer League (*ISL*) which enjoyed a few years of success as the only American league. When the *USSF* granted exclusive franchise rights to the United States Soccer Association (USSA) to organize another league, the ISL merged with another startup league to form the National Professional Soccer League (*NPSL*). The USSA and NPSL, competing heavily for the U.S. soccer audience, struggled until 1967 when they merged into one organization, the North American Soccer League (*NASL*). The NASL nearly folded in 1969, but through the tireless efforts of the league's founders, it began to grow steadily in the early 1970s.

A few events gave the NASL a much-needed boost. First, American interest in soccer was revived by an encouraging performance by the U.S. Olympic team at the 1972 Summer Olympics. The team made it through the rigorous qualifying process for the first time since 1956, although it was eliminated in the second round. Then, in 1973 an American named Kyle Rote Jr. won the NASL Rookie of the Year Award in a league dominated by foreign players. Increasing popularity allowed the NASL to become a truly national league, reaching 20 teams by 1975, including teams in New York and on the West Coast.

The year 1975 was a landmark one for soccer in the U.S. The New York Cosmos gave the NASL an enormous boost when it signed retired Brazilian great *Pelé* to a 3-year, $4.7 million contract, an amount nearly equal to all the other player salaries in the league combined. Through this single act, the Cosmos and the NASL became instant international celebrities. Soon, other international stars joined Pelé on the Cosmos, such as Germany's *Franz Beckenbauer* and Italy's *Giorgio Chinaglia*.

The league and U.S. soccer reaped immediate benefits. Attendance more than tripled to over 3.5 million fans per year as huge crowds paid to get a glimpse of these stars. The Cosmos themselves averaged over 35,000 fans per game. The pinnacle came in 1977 when, in Pelé's final season, the largest U.S. soccer crowd ever, over 77,000 cheering fans, saw the Cosmos win a *playoff* game on their way to the league championship.

Unfortunately for the league and U.S. soccer fans, this success was fleeting. After Pelé's retirement and the departure of other key stars, attendance quickly dropped to its former levels. The league could not support as many teams, shrinking from 24 teams in 1977 to 9 teams only a few years later. The NASL became solely an indoor league before it finally folded in 1985.

Another indoor soccer league did much better — the Major Indoor Soccer League (*MISL*) started up in 1977, introducing a game played on a modified hockey rink covered by artificial turf by 2 teams of 6 players each. Because its games were higher-scoring and faster-paced than outdoor soccer, the MISL survived through the 1980s, becoming the Major Soccer League (*MSL*) in 1990. The MSL folded in 1992.

TODAY'S U.S. SOCCER
Other professional leagues replaced the NASL, although they have not achieved nearly the same popularity. Today, the best soccer in the U.S. is played at the collegiate level and in 2 small professional leagues:

- American Professional Soccer League (*APSL*): Sanctioned by the USSF as the nation's only outdoor professional soccer league, it played a full schedule for the first time in 1991. It plays by the *FIFA Laws of the Game* on grass *fields*. The APSL consists of 8 teams sprinkled throughout the U.S. and Canada (expanding to 12 in 1995) and plays its games in the spring and summer. Strict rules require the teams to be comprised mostly of American players — only 2 non-Americans are allowed on each team's active roster.

- National Professional Soccer League (*NPSL*): An indoor league of 12 teams that plays its games from October through April in modified hockey rinks, much like the former MISL. Many of the traditional rules of soccer have been altered to create a faster-paced, higher-scoring game. Points are assigned in a multiple scoring system like basketball, with 1, 2 and 3-*point* plays. The league's annual attendance has grown to over 1.5 million fans, a record for it but a mere fraction of that attained by other major sports leagues.

As a condition to FIFA's awarding it the 1994 games, the U.S. promised to organize a professional soccer league. A group headed by USSF President *Alan Rothenberg* is starting Major League Soccer (*MLS*) beginning in the spring of 1995. The league, containing 12 teams under centralized ownership, will try to instill greater national interest by requiring teams be composed mostly of American players like in the APSL. This restriction would be a significant change since most of today's great American-born players play professionally overseas, where there is greater competition and financial reward.

The MLS has FIFA's consent to experiment with elements of the game to attract American audiences. Traditionalists worry that rule changes, such as enlarging the goal to increase scoring, will ruin the essence of soccer.

NATIONAL SOCCER HALL OF FAME

American soccer of today and yesterday is on display at the National Soccer Hall of Fame in Oneonta, New York, where visitors are treated to the historical National Soccer Museum and the expansive 61-acre Wright National Soccer Campus. The mission of the Hall is to document, preserve and promote U.S. soccer and its history.

In the museum, the national archives of American soccer are displayed including old uniforms and equipment, photographs of the world's top players and other exhibits tracing the history of the game. There is also a video and reference library. The Campus includes 4 regulation-sized outdoor soccer *fields* where tournaments are played each summer at the youth, high school and collegiate levels.

The Hall originally opened in 1982 in a small mansion in Oneonta, and in 1987 moved to a temporary location downtown where it remains today. A larger permanent facility is being constructed on the Wright Campus that includes a 27,000-square foot participatory museum, 8 regulation soccer fields, a 10,000-seat stadium and an indoor arena. The Campus will serve national and international-level events.

As of 1993, a total of 197 individuals who contributed to soccer in the U.S. have been honored as inductees into the Hall. The first members were named by the Philadelphia Old-Timers' Association in 1950. Today, new members are inducted each June during National Soccer Hall of Fame Week, chosen by the *USSF*, the National Soccer Coaches Athletic Association (*NSCAA*) and the National Intercollegiate Soccer Officials of America Association.

SOCCER'S PERSONALITIES AND STARS

The biographies in this section are divided into 2 separate sections. First you will be introduced to some of the great international players of the past and present, and then you will meet some of the personalities involved with the United States' 1994 *World Cup* effort.

In the sport of soccer a player is permitted to join the *national team* in his native country to play in the World Cup and in other international tournaments. This does not prevent that same person from being under contract to play for a *league* in a different country <u>at the same time</u>. For example: an Italian citizen playing for a *club* in the Spanish League most of the year can win a European Cup with that team and also be invited to temporarily represent Italy in the World Cup. After the tournament, this player would continue playing for his Spanish club.

The following key abbreviations apply to the entries that follow:

(A)=Active Player
American Footballer of the Year =Best player in North, South & Central America
Bundesliga = the German professional soccer league
Caps = international appearances
Div. = Division
EUFA Cup = European Union Football Association Cup
FA Cup = England's Football Association Championship
FIFA World Player of the Year = an international award
Golden Ball = given to the *European Footballer of the Year*
Golden Boot = given to Europe's top scorer
Hermann Trophy = Best U.S. Collegiate Player of the Year
MAC Award = Missouri Athletic Club Collegiate Soccer Player of the Year (U.S.)
MVP = Most Valuable Player
NASL = *North American Soccer League* (now defunct)
NSCAA = National Soccer Coaches Association of America
Prem. = Premier
Soccer Bowl = NASL championship

INTERNATIONAL PLAYERS: PAST & PRESENT

Baggio, Roberto: (*Striker, Midfielder*) (A) He is the man Italy is expecting to lead it to an unprecedented fourth World Cup victory in 1994. The most expensive soccer player in the world, this pony-tailed, 27-year old Italian is nicknamed "the laser." *Pelé* considers him the heir apparent to *Diego Maradona* (who has been considered the world's best player since Pelé reigned from 1958-1970), believing this nimble youth will only get better. A record $13.8 million was paid in 1990 for his reluctant transfer from Florence to Juventus (Italian 1st Div.) which caused 2 days of rioting in Florence.

He proved his worth by becoming the *league's* second highest *scorer* with 17 goals in his first season. Despite this, he never led a team to a championship until he took Juventus to victory in the 1993 *EUFA Cup*. As a reward, Baggio will receive a reported $2.5 million annually through 1996. In 1993, he was named both *FIFA World Player of the Year* and *European Footballer of the Year*. Baggio studies Buddhism and practices meditation, which his mother, a practicing Catholic, has some trouble accepting.

Beckenbauer, Franz: (*Sweeper, Midfielder*) "Kaiser Franz", as he is affectionately known, is one of the rare individuals to win a World Cup both as a player and a coach. This German superstar

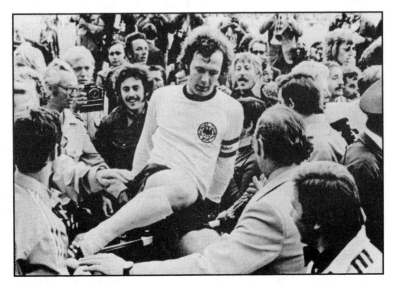

is said to have often left the *field* with his shirt looking as ironed as when the game started, seeming not to have broken a sweat. Gifted with incredible physical and mental control and coordination, he revolutionized the sweeper position, turning it into more of an *offensive* weapon. His elegant footwork and long accurate *passes* looked effortless and unhurried. To *Johan Cruyff*, he is "the greatest player in football history." No one disagrees that he is the greatest West German player of all time. The only criticism leveled against him was that his coolness hinted of arrogance.

This son of a postman aspired to selling insurance but instead he joined the *club* FC Bayern, Munich at the age of 18, leading it to become one of the most feared in Europe. Beckenbauer first earned international acclaim in the 1966 World Cup, when he was only 20 years old and his West German *national team* lost in the finals against England and *Bobby Charlton*. Since then, he captained the 1974 World Cup championship team, was named *European Footballer of the Year* twice (1972, 1976), captained Bayern to 3 consecutive European Cup victories (1974-1976), led Bayern to 4 *Bundesliga* championships and 4 German Cups, won the World Club Cup (1976), the European Cup Winner's Cup, the U.S. Championship, the American Footballer of the Year award, the *NASL MVP* of the Year award (1977) and 8 domestic German trophies including German Footballer of the Year in 1966, 1968, 1974 and 1976. Altogether, he amassed a record 103 *caps* for his country.

Incredibly, in 1977 he was converted to midfielder when he came to the U.S. to join the Cosmos (NASL) for $2.8 million over 4 years. In 1984, he left behind the comfort of retirement and lucrative endorsement contracts to begin a pressure-filled 6-year career as West Germany's trainer, helping to rebuild the team. In 1990, he finally succeeded by leading West Germany to their third World Cup title.

He later returned to his old club, Bayern, first in the role of vice-president and then, as of January 1994, as its coach. He was an early candidate for the position of coaching the U.S. national team in the 1994 World Cup, ultimately given to *Bora Milutinovic*. He has also been generous with money and time in his involvement with a charity he founded for the handicapped.

Bergkamp, Dennis: (*Striker*) (A) This tall, blonde, handsome 25-year old Dutchman is currently the most coveted young talent in Europe and a goal-scoring genius. With the heir-apparent to *Marco van Basten* on their side, some believe the Netherlands could well win the 1994 World Cup. In early 1993, Bergkamp surprised everyone when he left the Dutch *club* Ajax Amsterdam (where he started his career in 1981 as an apprentice) for Internazionale Milan when that club agreed to let him start every game and to alter its style of play.

He was a contender for the *FIFA World Player of the Year* award twice, coming in third behind *Roberto Baggio* and *Romario* in 1993 and behind teammate van Basten in 1992. He was also named the 1991-92 Dutch Player of the Year. All this after not even being selected to his country's 1990 World Cup team. Through dedication, he developed into a prolific *scorer*, amassing 83 goals in the next 3 seasons with Ajax compared with a meager 20 goals in his first 4 seasons with the club. He has earned 26 *caps* and scored 16 goals for the *national team*.

Best, George: (*Winger*) "Bestie" arrived in Manchester, England in 1961 as a 15-year old lad from Belfast and became one of the greatest British wingers of all time. *Pelé* once considered him "the greatest soccer player the world has ever seen", and every emerging young star is inevitably touted as the "new George Best." Although his greed for the ball was seen as a flaw, his outstanding *dribbling* and *goal scoring* made up for it. Yet, for all his talent, Best never appeared in a World Cup final. From 1963-1974 he played for Manchester United where his brilliant and flashy play helped it win 2 *league* championships and the European Cup in 1968, the same year he was named the *European Footballer of the Year*.

Some felt he epitomized the 1960s decade and its dream of freedom. Easily recognized as the only soccer player of his time to wear his hair long, Best led a controversial and flamboyant life full of gambling, womanizing and drinking, which contributed to the early demise of his career and earned him the title of "soccer's playboy." When he left Manchester in 1974 he was only 27 and in his prime. He attempted a series of shortlived comebacks, including one in the U.S. with 3 teams in the *NASL* from 1976-1983 and another in 1983, at the age of 37, as the lowest-paid player in England's 3rd Div.

83

Charlton, Bobby: (*Left Wing, Midfielder*) This English star, who started his illustrious career as a left wing, was the key midfielder to his country's 1966 World Cup victory. He was a soccer genius, known for his mastery of 20-yard thumps into the goal. Altogether, he won 106 *caps* for England and made over 600 appearances for Manchester United. Charlton scored twice in England's 1968 defeat of Portugal's Benfica in the European Cup. He was once named the *European Footballer of the Year* and long held the record for goals by an English player (49) set in 1970. After several failed coaching attempts, he concentrated his efforts on Bobby Charlton Enterprises, creating a flourishing international soccer instructional camp business. Today, he is one of soccer's most knowledgeable and celebrated ambassadors.

Chinaglia, Giorgio: (*Striker*) This Italian-born master goal *scorer* played for the New York Cosmos of the *NASL* from 1976 through 1983 and was the *league's* all-time leading scorer with 235 goals (in 243 games). He was compared to a snake striking its prey because his slow, tired appearance on the *field* would suddenly and surprisingly be punctuated by bursts of quickness. He holds every NASL outdoor scoring record including career goals (155) and playoff goals (44), and he led the NASL in scoring for 4 of his first 6 seasons (1976, 1978, 1980 and 1981). As the Cosmo's captain, he led them to 4 NASL *Soccer Bowl* championships (1977, 1978, 1980 and 1982) and was named player of the game in 2 of those finals. Despite being the highest scorer for the most successful team in the NASL, it was not until his 6th season in 1981 that he was named the league's *MVP*. When the NASL ceased operations in 1984 and the Cosmos joined the *MISL*, he acquired a 60% interest in the team and became its president. However, financial difficulties plagued the *club*, and a year later he left the organization to spend more time in Rome with Lazio, a team he owned in the Italian league.

Chinaglia began playing soccer at the age of 15 while growing up as an Italian immigrant in Wales. He went on to become one of the highest-paid players in the Italian league, playing 6 years for Lazio and leading that team to a national championship in 1974. In that same year he played for Italy in the World Cup. He was a volatile, controversial and outspoken player who shocked his fans when he left to play in the U.S. In America, he was often booed by Italian fans who were still angry over his defection to the U.S. and by others who accused him of scoring "garbage" goals, getting all the glory for scoring while barely acknowledging the hard work of teammates.

Cruyff, Johan: (*Midfielder, Striker*) A magician without great quickness or strength, Cruyff was considered one of the world's greatest soccer player after *Pelé* retired, winning a championship in every *league* he has played in. His greatest fault is that he talks too much (his nickname is the "Talking Machine") whether it be to his teammates, opponents or *referees*.

His career began at the age of 10 when he joined Ajax Amsterdam with whom he signed his first professional contract 5 years later, earning $20 a week to help support his widowed mother. Over the next 7 years, he led his team to 4 Dutch Cup titles (3 consecutive 1971-73) and 6 Dutch League crowns. His ability to set up goals from all over the *field* brought his native Holland (for whom he was captain) to the 1974 World Cup finals, where, despite the loss to West Germany, he was named outstanding player of the tournament and appeared on the cover of Time magazine. Altogether, he was *capped* 48 times for Holland and was named *European Footballer of the Year* an unprecedented 3 times (1971, 1973 and 1974).

In 1973, he requested to be sold to FC Barcelona (to avoid Holland's 80% tax rate) where he helped it win the Spanish League title in 1974 and became a national hero. This act of desertion was not taken lightly by Dutch fans who threw stones into the windows of the home of Cruyff's in-laws and mailed Cruyff a box containing a scorpion. In 1979, at the age of 32, he joined the *NASL*. He then returned to Holland and won another Dutch championship before retiring for good. Then he turned to coaching, for which he was offered upwards of $11,000 a game. As its advisor, he led his old team Ajax to a Cup Winners' Cup in 1987 and a European Cup victory in 1988. In 1991, this former chain-smoker suffered a coronary and had a double bypass operation at the young age of 44. He recovered and is currently the coach of the 1992 European championship team, FC Barcelona.

Eusebio (da Silva Ferreira): (*Striker*) In 1992, Portugal honored this legend with a special award as the greatest player in that country's history and in the same year, for his 50th birthday, erected a bronze statue of him at the entrance to Benfica's Stadium of Light in Lisbon. Only *Pelé* could match his international popularity. He was discovered playing barefoot in his native Mozambique and nicknamed the "Black Panther" for his uncanny ability to pounce on a loose ball and hammer it into the goal. Eusebio stole the show as the leading *scorer* of the 1966 World Cup (9 goals) despite Portugal's third-place finish. He was awarded the inaugural European *Golden Boot* as Europe's highest scorer in 1968, accomplishing the feat again in 1973.

In his 15-year playing career with Benfica that ended in 1975, he led the team to 2 European Cup victories in 1961 and 1962, 8 *league* championships and 5 Portuguese Cups. Of his 1,000+ career goals, his record of 46 goals for Benfica in the European Cup will not soon be broken. Altogether he has earned 64 Portuguese *caps*. He was one of the original stars in the *NASL* (1975-78) before Pelé, *Beckenbauer* and *Cruyff*, where until the age of 39, he provided offensive firepower to a number of teams and even led the Toronto Metros Croatia to the *Soccer Bowl* title in 1976. He returned to Portugal to coach, train, scout and act as ambassador for Benfica in 1991, maintaining a 30-year affiliation with the *club* that continues today.

Maradona, Diego: (*Midfielder*) (A) Despite being one of soccer's most tempestuous and controversial stars, he was considered the world's best soccer player in the 1980s. He is credited with repeatedly taking ordinary teams and making them great. No one can forget how, as its captain in 1986, he single-handedly led Argentina to its second World Cup in 8 years with his infamous "Hand of God" goal against England (although he disappointed fans by failing to score a single goal in 7 games during the 1990 World Cup). This stocky Argentine was voted Footballer of the Year 4 times by the World Newspaper (1979, 1980, 1986 and 1989). With Napoli (Italian 1st Div.) he achieved god-like status for leading the *club* to a *EUFA Cup* and its only 2 *league* titles in 4 years, earning $2-3 million per season.

Yet, the 33-year old "king" of soccer lived up to his early reputation as a delinquent, bringing a career fraught with controversy and brattish antics to a head with his 15-month international suspension for cocaine possession and drug-trafficking charges in Italy and Argentina in 1991. The scandals in Maradona's life seem endless: a paternity suit filed in 1986, a lawsuit by Napoli seeking damages caused to its image by his misbehavior in 1990 followed by the team's attempt to drop him from the squad entirely in 1991 (he was traded to Sevilla of Spain for a $15 million transfer fee in late 1992), and most recently criticism for autographing his shirt for Cuban dictator Fidel Castro in 1993. Assorted squabbles have developed with just about every team he has ever played for: he remains bitter for his exclusion from the 1978 Argentine *national team* when he was a teenage phenomenon; in 1991 he vowed never to play for his country again unless he received an apology for double dealing by Argentine soccer federation officials; and in 1993 he was fined for making critical remarks about the Spanish Soccer Federation and for fighting during a *match*.

He has announced his resignation from soccer numerous times, yet the saga continues. Now in the 19th year of his career, Maradona is back in Argentina playing for the unpopular 1st Div. Newell's Old Boys and he is likely to appear for his fourth World Cup in 1994.

Matthews, Stanley (Sir): *(Winger)* Considered one of the best English wingers of all time and one of the most celebrated soccer stars of his era, the "wizard of *dribble*" was the first soccer player ever knighted for his performance on the *field*. His playing days, which lasted until he was in his 50s, began in 1930 when he was 15. He stayed with the same small-town team for most of his career. Sir Matthews took part in 2 World Cups but is best remembered for his brilliant shattering of *defenses* in the 1953 English *FA Cup* final, known as the "Matthews Final." In his 34-year career he earned 54 full English *caps*. In 84 games for England, he never received a single *caution*, and in 1986 was awarded an international trophy for fair play. In 1970, he retired from soccer to pursue his business interests, although he continued to coach teams from San Francisco to Soweto, South Africa into his 70s.

Milla, Roger: *(Striker)* He was crowned a tribal prince in Kumba for his role as Cameroon's World Cup 1990 hero when at the age of 39 he defied 500-1 odds and led his "Indomitable Lions" to the *quarterfinals*. A continent-wide celebration erupted as it was the first time an African nation advanced so far in the tournament. Even *FIFA* was impressed, increasing Africa's 1994

World Cup berths from 2 to 3. Milla became the oldest *scorer* in World Cup history and delighted fans with his hip-wiggling jigs (similar to a lambada) by the *corner flag* after each goal. Interestingly, he had been invited to the 1990 team by a presidential decree to impart the wisdom of age, over the objections of a national coach who thought him too old. Even Milla's acceptance came with reluctance — he had quit the team when his national federation failed to care for his dying mother while the team was playing abroad. In 1990, he was voted African Footballer of the Year and named Male Sports Personality of the Year by the Village Voice.

He grew up kicking lemons and rags tied together into balls down the streets of Yaounde. Before leaving to play in France at the age of 25, he had already achieved the title of Africa's best player. His first appearance for Cameroon's *national team* was in 1976, and he played a key role in both its 1984 (leading scorer of the tournament) and 1988 Africa Nations Cup victories. In 1989, after a distinguished 17-year career, he retired from soccer for the first time, moving to the secluded island of La Reunion to play for an amateur team.

In 1992, he tried to organize a charity competition involving pygmy soccer players in an effort to bring attention to their plight and earn money for health and education facilities. However, controversy ensued when it was discovered the pygmies had been left locked in the stadium basement for days with little to eat. Milla will coach Cameroon in the 1994 World Cup, and at the insistence of his country's president and the American organizers, this 43-year old may even consider playing in the tournament.

Moore, Bobby: (*Sweeper*) The "golden boy of English soccer" captained England to its only World Cup title in 1966 and was voted player of the tournament. The year after, he was honored by the Queen when he was awarded an OBE. *Pelé* described him as "the world's greatest *defender*" and he is considered the best captain England has ever had. Moore was the perfect English gentleman. Over a 20-year career in England, he appeared in 3 World Cups and earned 108 *caps* (a record that stood until 1978). In his 90 senior appearances for England, the team lost only 13 games.

Moore began his 30-year career at the age of 16 and signed his first professional contract with West Ham United a year later in 1958. During his 15 years with West Ham, his team won the *FA Cup* (1964) and the European Cup Winner's Cup (1965), and he was crowned *European Footballer of the Year* (1964). He played over 1,000 games for West Ham and his subsequent *club*, Fulham.

Oddly, this distinguished gentleman was accused of stealing an emerald bracelet he could have purchased with loose change while playing in Bogota, Columbia in 1970, an event that escalated into an international incident. His team was forced to leave him under house arrest and go off to the World Cup in Mexico without him. He was later permitted to join his teammates and his name was eventually cleared in what many thought was a frame-up. In 1977, he left England for the U.S. where he played in the *NASL*, and then coached in Hong Kong briefly. However, managerial success eluded him. In February 1993, just 9 days after he made the news of his illness public, Moore died at the age of 51 after a 2-year battle with liver cancer.

Pelé: (*Forward*) This Brazilian legend is easily soccer's greatest star and probably the most recognizable athlete in the soccer world. In Brazil they call him the "Black Pearl", in Chile he is the "Dangerous One" and in Italy, he is the "King." So rare is his skill, that in 1960, the Brazilian government voted him a national

treasure to ensure he would not be sold to a *club* outside the country. Now, at the age of 54, Pelé is playing the role of the sport's greatest ambassador. In his travels, he has met over 88 heads of state including 5 U.S. Presidents.

It is unclear why childhood friends gave Edson Arantes do Nascimento the nickname of Pelé as they kicked a rag-stuffed sock down cobblestoned alleys. He did not like it at first — his family still calls him Dico. This son of a professional soccer player must have been born with the sport in his blood. His youth team won 3 consecutive championships leading him to sign his first professional contract with the powerful Santos FC in his native São Paolo at the age of 15. It was the only Brazilian club he would play for in his 22-year career. Within 2 years he was the *league's* leading *scorer*, setting a record with 53 goals in 1957.

The growing international reputation of its star player made Santos the world's most highly sought-after team, and by Pelé's retirement in 1974, the club had played in 65 different nations. The war in Biafra was actually halted for 3 days when Pelé came to play, and he was made a knight of the Order of Merit by Charles de Gaulle, president of France. Back at home, for every "special" goal Pelé scored (those requiring extraordinary skill and athleticism) avid fans would mount a plaque in the stadium. His athletic ability, peripheral vision and ball control provided him with precious extra seconds during which he would outsmart his opponents (in 1,363 *matches* he scored 1,282 goals). Along with the many matches where he scored 3 or 4 goals, he amassed an incredible 5 goals on 6 occasions and even 8 in one game!

He is also remembered for his 4 consecutive trips to the World Cup with the Brazilian *national team*, which resulted in 3 championships (1958, 1962 and 1970). He remains the only player with 3 World Cup victories to his name. His last international match was in 1971 and his final appearance for Santos came 3 years later. But Pelé's first retirement did not last long.

In 1975, when the New York Cosmos of the *NASL* beckoned, he came to the U.S to play, popularizing the game virtually single-handedly. In 1976 he was named the league's *MVP*, and the next year he led the Cosmos to the *Soccer Bowl* championship. His final game in New York in 1977 (against his former club Santos) drew nearly 76,000 fans. Fittingly, he was inducted into the U.S. *National Soccer Hall of Fame* in 1993. The world was recently shocked when Pelé's feud with fellow Brazilian João Havelange, the 77-year old president of *FIFA*, led Havelange to deny Pelé participation in the 1993 World Cup *Draw*. Today Pelé still lives in New York, an outspoken proponent of rule changes to make soccer more exciting for spectators, a charming and gracious individual who always finds time to sign autographs for children. He has even considered running for President of Brazil in 1995 on a health and education reform platform.

Platini, Michel: (*Midfielder*) Considered one of the most brilliant players of his generation and the most popular sports hero in France, his command of the *midfield* in the late 1970s allowed France to emerge as a world soccer power. He captained the French *national team* to a European Championship in 1984 and to 2 World Cup *semifinals* in 1982 and 1986. With 41 goals in 71 international appearances, he remains to this day the highest *scorer* in French history. This uncanny creator was also the most dangerous player off of a *direct free kick*, earning him the nickname "Mr. Free Kick" for his ability to *hook* a ball around a *wall* of players. Yet his main talent was not scoring, but playmaking.

Platini was named *European Footballer of the Year* 3 consecutive times (1983, 1984 and 1985), tying a record set by *Johan Cruyff*. He led Juventus (Italian 1st Div.) to 3 consecutive Italian *league* titles (1983-85), the 1984 Cup Winner's Cup (setting an European Cup record with 9 goals) and the 1985 European Champion Clubs' Cup. In 1985 he received France's highest honor, the Legion d'Honneur.

In 1987, at the age of 32, he retired from soccer, but one year later he returned to coach the French national team. His managerial career had a shaky start, but he led that team to a 3-year unbeaten run from 1990-92, after which he retired. In 1988, he was awarded a medal by Jordan's King Hussein for his efforts in battling drug abuse. He is currently the co-president of the 1998 World Cup to be held in France and a member of Task Force 2000, a committee studying ways to improve the game for spectators.

Romario (de Souza Faria): (*Striker*) (A) A fiery and
temperamental Brazilian from Rio de Janeiro with an instinct for
scoring, he was the top individual *scorer* at the 1984 Olympic
Games (7 goals) and scored over 200 goals in his first 3 seasons
as a professional. Rio's Vasca de Gama *club* sold him to PSV
Eindhoven of the Netherlands for $4.7 million in 1988 which
made the 22-year old an instant millionaire. He led the *league* in
scoring in each of his first 3 seasons. In 1993 he moved to FC
Barcelona (Spain) under coach *Johan Cruyff* and was a finalist for
the *FIFA World Player of the Year* award. He was second only to
Baggio in voting for *European Footballer of the Year* in 1993.

Interestingly enough, this goal-scoring machine has rarely been
called upon to play for the Brazilian *national team* — he was
dropped for disciplinary reasons in 1986 and for an injury before
the 1990 World Cup. His juvenile and egotistical behavior has
caused this mercurial star to be at odds with virtually every
manager he has played under — leading him to be dubbed the
Brazilian *Maradona*. His scoring has been inconsistent at times,
but even *Pelé* believes his country's success in World Cup 1994
hinges on Romario, the nation's best player and most dangerous
weapon. Though clearly at the peak of his game, the 28-year old
Romario has stated that he plans to retire soon. For him the only
challenge remaining is to play in the World Cup.

Rossi, Paolo: (*Striker*) This black-maned Italian, who made a
name for himself with his heroic 1982 World Cup exploits and
for his breathtaking tactical intelligence, has experienced a career
of highs and lows. After a 2-year suspension for his alleged
involvement in a 1980 bribery and betting scandal that shook the
Italian *League*, he returned to Juventus (1st. Div.) in 1982 at the
age of 25. He returned to the Italian *national team* that same year
and led it to its third World Cup championship with an
incredible 3-game, 6-goal scoring spree (including a *hat trick*
against Brazil), making him the World Cup's top *scorer* and a
national hero. For his efforts he was voted *European Footballer of
the Year* and Soccer Player of the Year by World Soccer Magazine,
promised free shoes for life and given the Italian equivalent of
knighthood. The next year, however, his scoring for both
Juventus and the national team decreased dramatically, leading
to his exclusion from the 1986 World Cup team. In 1987, when
his only offer came from a Turkish 1st Div. *club*, he decided to
retire at the age of 31.

Van Basten, Marco: (*Striker*) (A) One of the world's leading *offensive* players, he rose from the operating table after ankle surgery to become the leading *scorer* in the Netherlands' 1988 European Cup victory. He is a complete player, a natural who has been compared to *Diego Maradona* and *Michel Platini* by those who have coached him. This 30-year old Dutchman was named *European Footballer of the Year* in 1992 for the third time, tying a record set by his mentor and coach *Johan Cruyff* and matched only by Platini. Van Basten then spent the next 18 months recuperating from another ankle injury.

His records include scoring 218 goals in 280 *matches* with Ajax Amsterdam (where he began his career at the age of 17 as a *substitute* for Cruyff) and AC Milan with whom he is currently under contract for $2 million+ a year through 1996. Unfortunately, the world's best goal scorer is unlikely to have any impact on the 1994 World Cup because he is recuperating from yet another recent ankle surgery.

1994 WORLD CUP: U.S. PLAYERS & PERSONALITIES

Caligiuri, Paul: (*Midfielder*) (A) In 1990, he was responsible for the U.S. qualifying for its first World Cup appearance in 40 years when he scored "the shot heard around the world", the only goal in a *qualifying match* against Trinidad & Tobago. Then, during the tournament, he made history again when he scored the first American World Cup goal since 1940 against Czechoslovakia. Caligiuri was one of the first U.S. players to go overseas, where he played with several German teams before returning to America in 1991. This native Californian was a member of the *starting* team at the 1988 Summer Olympics in South Korea. In 1985, he captained the UCLA team that won the *NCAA* championship. His father, Bob, has been this 30-year old's personal coach since he was 7 years old.

Dooley, Thomas: (*Defender, Midfielder*) (A) He is a versatile *defensive midfielder* who can also play *sweeper* or *forward*. This 33-year old was born and raised in Germany. He played professionally in Germany's *Bundesliga* — for 5 years at Homburg and then for 1st Div. FC Kaiserslautern where he was voted team *MVP* in Germany's 1991 championship game. Because his father was an American serviceman stationed overseas, he was able to have a U.S. passport reissued in 1992, even though he had not seen his now-deceased father in over 30 years. This enabled Dooley to join the U.S. *national team,* fulfilling his quest to play international soccer since he was never selected for the German national team. He has studied enough architecture to design his own home.

Friedel, Brad: (*Goalkeeper*) (A) His stunning saves helped the U.S. team bring home its first-ever gold medal for soccer from the Pan American Games in the summer of 1991. Originally from Bay Village, Ohio, this 23-year old was also a member of UCLA's 1990 *NCAA* championship team, a 3-time All-American and considered one of the best goalkeepers in UCLA's history. In 1992, he represented the U.S. at the Olympics and was named Goalkeeper of the Year. The next year, while still a junior at UCLA, he won the *Hermann Trophy* and the Adidas Goalkeeper of the Year award. Most noted for his composure and confidence in the *net*, he is expected to challenge *Tony Meola* for the *starting* position in the 1994 World Cup. In high school, he was a 3-sport athlete (soccer, basketball and tennis) who was invited to try out as a walk-on to UCLA's basketball team.

Harkes, John: (*Midfielder*) (A) One of the best products of the U.S. youth soccer system, this 27-year old son of Scottish immigrants, currently plays professionally overseas for Derby County in the English 1st Div. Originally from Kearny, New Jersey, he brought worldwide respect to American soccer players in 1993 by becoming not only the first American to play in an *FA Cup* final at England's famed Wembley Stadium, but the first American to score a goal during an FA Cup final. Along the way, Harkes helped his team, Sheffield Wednesday, advance from the 2nd to the 1st to the Prem. Div. and capture the 1991 English *League* Cup championship before his $300,000 contract expired in 1993. He is considered the most successful U.S. player to join a foreign professional league. In 1987 he was honored with the *MAC Award.* He is the U.S. team's resident comedian with a knack for imitating foreign accents.

Jones, Cobi N'Gai: (*Midfielder*) (A) In 1988, as a freshman at UCLA, this walk-on earned a scholarship and worked his way into the Bruins' *starting* lineup just 7 games into the season. Two years later he helped lead UCLA to the *NCAA* championship, and in the summer of 1991 joined his U.S. teammates in bringing home the country's first gold medal for soccer from the Pan American games. He started for the U.S. team in the 1992 Olympics, making his mark as the team's most dynamic player and garnering substantial publicity for sharing the same first name as the official *mascot* of the Barcelona games, Cobi the Dog. After the Olympics, Jones signed up with the struggling German 1st Div. *club*, FC Cologne. The 24-year old from Westlake Village, California wears dreadlocks and is noted for his incredible speed. He is the player on the U.S. team who has developed the most in the last 6 years.

Keller, Kasey: (*Goalkeeper*) (A) This 24-year old from Olympia, Washington is fast becoming one of the best goalkeepers in Europe, where he currently plays professionally as a *starter* for Milwall (England 1st Div.) With over 16 *shutouts* and 49 consecutive starts in 1993, he was instrumental in Milwall's quest for a promotion to the Prem. Div. Keller was a member of both the under-16 and under-20 U.S. *national teams*. He was also a 3-time All-American at the University of Portland and helped lead his team to the *NCAA* Final Four as a freshman. He may challenge *Tony Meola* for the position of starting *goalie* in the 1994 World Cup.

Lalas, Alexi: (*Sweeper*) (A) From Birmingham, Michigan, this 24-year old sports a mop of red hair and an elongated goatee. In 1991 he won the *Hermann Trophy* and was selected for the *MAC Award*. He captained the team at Rutgers in his 3 years there (while pursuing an English major) *starting* in 80 of 81 games. Lalas was a member of the 1992 U.S. Olympic team that played at Barcelona. His goals tend to come off of *set plays* (*corner kicks* or *free kicks*) as he is good at *heading* the ball into the *net*. Opponents will unfortunately find him particularly adept at elbowing, a skill he learned as a high school hockey star when he took his team to the state title. Lalas' other love is music; he plays acoustic guitar, writes songs and devotes much of his time to the band "The Gypsies" which plays in New York clubs.

Meola, Tony: (*Goalkeeper*) (A) One of the top-rated U.S. players, he *started* all 3 games for the U.S. in the 1990 World Cup but was nevertheless refused a work permit to play in England. He played for the Fort Lauderdale Strikers of the *APSL* instead. Meola also played *goalie* for the undefeated U.S. team in its 1992 U.S. Cup championship. In 1993, he led the U.S. team to the *semifinals* in the *CONCACAF* Gold Cup and was voted the U.S. Cup's top goalkeeper for his spectacular play in the 2-0 win against England.

This 25-year old son of a barber (and a former professional Italian soccer player), from Kearny, New Jersey has always been an all-around athlete. When he had 43 *shutouts* in his first 3 seasons for his high school soccer team, he got bored, switched to playing *forward* in his senior year and scored 33 goals. At the same time, he was named All-State in baseball (he played third base in high school) and basketball (at 6'1" and 205 pounds, he makes dunking look easy). While at the University of Virginia, in addition to soccer he played center field and was drafted by the New York Yankees; his soccer playing earned him 2 *MAC Awards* (1987 and 1989) and a *Hermann Trophy* (1989). Despite being a starter since 1989, a 1990 World Cup veteran, the U.S. team's captain and currently its most recognizable and highest-paid member, Meola faces the constant challenge of keeping *Friedel* or *Keller* from taking over his position.

Milutinovic, Bora: (Coach, former *Midfielder*) This Yugoslavian-born head coach of the U.S. team since March 1991 prefers to conduct his post-game interviews in Spanish. Perhaps that is because he refers to himself as a "Yugoslav-Mexican" — he played soccer in Mexico for many years, married a Mexican woman and then guided the Mexican *national team* to the *quarterfinals* of the 1986 World Cup. For this accomplishment, he was honored with the highest award for a foreigner by the president of Mexico. After assorted managerial assignments, he coached Costa Rica in the 1990 World Cup, taking that team past the second *round* although he had begun his tenure with the team just 90 days before the tournament.

Despite an unkempt appearance accompanied by demonstrative and animated behavior, his coaching methods, referred to as "Milutinovich's cure", are designed to instill greater organization, running power and physical strength. Since both teams he led in the last 2 World Cups exceeded all expectations, and since he has already led the U.S. to some unprecedented international championships (1991 *CONCACAF* Gold Cup, 1992 U.S. Cup) there are high hopes that he can work his magic on the U.S. effort in 1994. He is the first coach in World Cup history to lead 3 national teams from different countries in successive tournaments. In his 50 years he has worked in 5 different countries and learned to speak 6 languages. His hobbies include reading psychology books and playing chess.

Ramos, Tab: (*Midfielder*) (A) Born in Uruguay to a professional soccer-playing father in 1963, this U.S. national from Hillside, New Jersey plays professionally overseas for Real Betis (Spain) where he is becoming a top-rated player. He is considered one of the most consistent players in the U.S., with creativity and a good sense for the game. This All-American from North Carolina State became a star in his 2 seasons with the *ASL*. His playing when he was just 13 years old inspired Rev. Leahy, the headmaster of St. Benedict's Prep (Newark, N.J.) to add soccer to the athletic program. Ten years later, in 1990, Ramo's alma mater won the high school national championship.

Reyna, Claudio: (*Midfielder*) (A) The list of awards and accolades received by this 20-year old from Springfield, New Jersey belies his age. He is the nation's best all-around player — a highly-skilled passer who never seems to hurry, he is also known for his vision, accuracy, pace, fluidity and ability to improvise in the *midfield*. His style has been compared to *Maradona's*, who happens to be Reyna's favorite player. Reyna's supercool image is enhanced by the diamond stud he wears in his right ear and the gold loop earring in his left. As the son of a former Argentine 1st Div. pro *forward* who came to the U.S. in 1968, Reyna was turned on to soccer at a very young age. At 17, he was the youngest member of the U.S. team that brought home the gold medal from the Pan American games in 1991 and the youngest member of the U.S. Olympic team in Barcelona in 1992 and he is likely to be the youngest player on the U.S. 1994 World Cup team.

While at New Jersey's St. Benedict's Prep he scored 62 goals and 59 assists in an undefeated (25-0) 3-year career that helped that school maintain a 47-game win streak. Reyna made his international debut just weeks after completing a 3-year college career at the University of Virginia that saw him win every award college soccer has to offer. Many agree he is probably the most talented individual to take part in the *NCAA* soccer tournament since its inception in 1959. In 3 years, Reyna led

Virginia to 3 consecutive NCAA championships (1991-1993), securing the team's place in the record books as the only Div. I team to accomplish the feat in the tournament's 35-year history. He was named freshman of the year by Soccer America, twice named Collegiate Player of the Year and was voted most outstanding *offensive player* in Virginia's 1991 and 1992 NCAA victories. In 1992, he was also named to the *NSCAA* All-American first team and was a finalist for the *Hermann Trophy*. He was the first male player to win the *MAC Award* in consecutive years. He won Div. I All-America honors for 3 straight years and won all 3 collegiate player of the year awards in 1993 before deciding to forego his senior year.

Reyna is likely to seek out a European contract after the 1994 World Cup. He already turned down one 4-year contract offered to him after participating in the 1992 Olympics to play for *Johan Cruyff*, coach of then-European champion FC Barcelona, opting instead to return to the University of Virginia.

Rothenberg, Alan: (*USSF* and World Cup 1994 President) This distinguished trial lawyer and sports executive has been involved with American soccer for over 25 years. He owned the Los Angeles Aztecs (*NASL*) and was general manager of the Los Angeles Wolves (United Soccer Association). Rothenberg was also responsible for soccer at the 1984 Olympics in Los Angeles which drew the largest crowds of any sport. He began his sports involvement as an advisor to Jack Kent Cooke (former owner of the Los Angeles Lakers, Los Angeles Kings, etc.). He was a member of the National Basketball Association's Board of Governors for 8 years and President of the Los Angeles Clippers for 7. He has been the President of the USSF since 1990 and is the Chairman, President and Chief Executive Officer of World Cup USA 1994, Inc. (the non-profit legal entity charged with staging the 1994 World Cup tournament under the direction of *FIFA*). He is expected to play a large role when the new American soccer *league*, the *MSL*, is founded in 1995.

Stewart, Ernie: (*Forward*) (A) This rising star plays professionally overseas for Willem II of the Netherlands 1st Div.

The 24-year old has great speed, enabling him to get *behind defenders*, and a gift for scoring goals. In the 1990-91 season he was the third-leading *scorer* in the Dutch *League* with 17 goals. Stewart, the son of an American serviceman stationed overseas, was born and raised in the Netherlands. Although he has lived there most of his life, the rules of international soccer permit him to play for the U.S. because he carries an American passport.

Wegerle, Roy: (*Forward*) (A) This 30-year old currently plays professionally overseas as a *starter* for Oldham (England Prem. Div.). Although born in South Africa, he received his U.S. citizenship in 1991 because he married an American and is therefore eligible to play for the U.S. Big-time scoring is the asset he brings to the U.S. team. He scored 10 goals in his final 13 games with Blackburn before being traded to Coventry City (Prem. Div.) in late March 1993 for $1.8 million. Wegerle attended the University of Southern Florida in 1982 and 1983 and played in both the *NASL* and *MISL*.

Wynalda, Eric: (*Forward*) (A) This 25-year old from Westlake Village, California is highly regarded as one of the most skilled young players in America. Currently, he plays professionally overseas for 1st Div. FC Saarbrucken in Germany. He was the first American to play in the German *Bundesliga* and is easily one of its most popular players. His team once sold 1,700 T-shirts with Wynalda's picture on it in 4 days (at $21 a shirt). He is such a recognized figure that he moved to France last year to escape the attention. In his first of 3 years at San Diego State, his team made it to the *NCAA* Final Four.

GLOSSARY

Advantage rule: a clause in the rules that directs the *referee* to refrain from stopping play for a *foul* if a stoppage would benefit the team that committed the violation.

Advantages or *breaks*: situations where a team has possession of the ball and outnumbers the opposition near the opposing *goal*.

American football: a term used by non-Americans to distinguish the popular U.S. sport of *football* from soccer which they also call football.

APSL: American Professional Soccer League — the nation's only outdoor professional soccer *league* since 1991, consisting of 8 teams in the U.S. and Canada (expanding to 12 by 1995).

Assist: the *pass* or passes which immediately precede a *goal*; a maximum of two assists can be credited for one goal.

Attacking midfielder: the most forward-playing *midfielder*, playing right behind the *forwards*; he supports the *offense* by providing passes to forwards to set up *goals*.

Attacker: any player on the team that has *possession* of the ball.

Attacking team: the team that has *possession* of the ball.

AYSO: American Youth Soccer Organization — an administrative body of youth soccer which sets rules and provides information and equipment to youth league *referees*, coaches and players.

Back: a *defender*.

Back header: a player's use of his head to direct the ball backwards.

Back tackle: an attempt by a *defender* to take the ball away from a *ball carrier* by swinging the defender's leg in front of the ball from behind.

Ball carrier: a player that has *possession* of the ball.

Banana kick or *hook*: a type of kick that gives the ball a curved trajectory; used to get the ball around an obstacle such as a *goaltender* or *defender*.

Beat: to get the *ball* through or around an opponent by *dribbling* or *shooting*.

100

Behind the defender: the area between a *defender* and his *goal*.

Bicycle kick or *scissors kick*: when a player kicks the ball in mid-air backwards and over his own head, usually making contact above waist level; an acrobatic shot.

Break: when a team quickly advances the ball down the *field* in an attempt to get its players near the opponent's *goal* before the *defenders* have a chance to retreat; also called an *advantage*.

Breakaway: when an *attacker* with the ball approaches the *goal* undefended; this exciting play pits a sole attacker against the *goalkeeper* in a one-on-one showdown.

Bundesliga: The German professional soccer *league*.

Cap: a recognition earned by a player for each appearance in an international game for his country.

Carrying the ball: a *foul* called on a *goalkeeper* when he takes more than 4 steps while holding or bouncing the ball.

Caution: see *Yellow card*.

Center: a *pass* from a player located near the *sideline* towards the middle of the *field*; used to get the ball closer to the front of the *goal*; also called a *cross*.

Center circle: a circular marking with a 10-yard radius in the center of the *field* from which *kickoffs* are taken to start or restart the game.

Center line: see *Midfield line*.

Center spot: a small circular mark inside the *center circle* that denotes the center of the *field* from which *kickoffs* are taken to start or restart the game.

Central defender: a player who guards the area directly in front of his own *goal* in a *zone defense*; does not exist in a *man-to-man* defense.

Charge: to run into an opponent; legal if done from the front or side of the *ball carrier*; illegal against a player without the ball or from behind.

Chest trap: when a player uses his chest to slow down and control a ball in the air.

Chip pass: a *pass lofted* into the air from a player to a teammate; used primarily to evade a *defender* by kicking the ball over his head.

Chip shot: a kick *lofted* into the air to try to sail the ball over the *goalkeeper's* head and still make it under the *crossbar* into the *goal*.

Clear: to kick the ball away from one's *goal*.

Cleats: the metal, plastic or rubber points in the bottom of a soccer shoe used to provide a player with traction; term also used to refer to the shoes themselves.

Club: a team that plays in a *league*.

CONCACAF: The Confederation Norte-Centroamericana y Del Caribe de Footbal — the regional organization of North American and Central American soccer under which *World Cup qualifying matches* are played; member countries include the U.S., Canada, Mexico, and Central American and Caribbean countries.

Consolation match: a tournament game played between the losers of the 2 *semifinal matches* to determine the third-place team.

Corner arc or *corner area*: a quarter-circle with a radius of 1 yard located at each of the 4 corners of the *field*; on a *corner kick*, the ball must be kicked from inside this arc.

Corner area: see *Corner arc*.

Corner flag: the flag located at each of the 4 corners of the *field*, inside the *corner area*.

Corner kick: a type of restart where the ball is kicked from the *corner arc* in an attempt to *score*; awarded to an *attacking team* when the ball crosses the *goal line* last touched by the *defending team*.

Counterattack: an attack launched by a *defending team* soon after it regains *possession* of the ball.

Creating space: when a player from the *attacking team* moves without the ball to draw *defenders* away from the *ball carrier* and give him space.

Cross or crossing pass: a *pass* from an *attacking player* near the *sideline* to a teammate in the middle or opposite side of the *field*; used to give the teammate a good *scoring opportunity*.

Crossbar: the horizontal beam that forms the top of a *goal* and sits on top of the two *posts*; it is 24 feet long and supported 8 feet above the ground.

Cut down the angle: when the *goalie* comes out of the *goal* several feet to make himself closer and larger to an *attacker*, leaving the attacker less *net* to shoot at.

Cut off: when a *defensive player* keeps his body between an *attacker* and the *defender's goal*, forcing the attacker out towards the *sidelines*.

Dangerous play: when a player attempts a play that the *referee* considers dangerous to that player or others, such as trying to kick the ball out of the *goalie's* hands, even if no contact is made.

Defenders: the players on the team that does not have *possession* of the ball.

Defending team: the team that does not have *possession* of the ball.

Defense: a team's function of preventing the opposition from scoring.

Defensemen: the 3 or 4 players on a team whose primary task is to stop the opposition from scoring; also called *fullbacks*.

Defensive midfielder: the player positioned just in front of his team's *defense*; he is often assigned to *mark* the opposition's best *offensive player*; also called the *midfield anchor*.

Defensive pressure: when one or more *defenders* closely *mark* a *ball carrier* to harass him into losing the ball.

Deflection: the ricochet of a ball after it hits a player.

Direct free kick: a kick awarded to a player for a serious *foul* committed by the opposition; the player kicks a stationary ball with no opposing players within 10 feet of him; a *goal* can be scored directly from this kick without the ball touching another player.

Diving header: a ball struck near ground level by the head of a diving player.

Draw: a game that ends with a *tied* score.

The Draw: the selection of *World Cup* teams to place them into playing groups for the tournament and the event surrounding this selection.

Dribbler: a player who advances the ball while controlling it with his feet.

Dribbling: the basic skill of advancing the ball with the feet while controlling it.

Drop ball: a method of restarting a game where the *referee* drops the ball between 2 players facing each other.

Drop kick: when a *goalie* drops the ball from his hands and kicks it before it hits the ground.

Endline: see *Goal line*.

English Football Association: an association of English soccer teams founded in 1863 to set soccer rules.

European Cup: the championship tournament played between Europe's top *national teams*.

F.A.: Football Association; often used to refer to the *English Football Association*, who, along with *FIFA* and other football associations, helps maintain the rules of soccer.

Fake or feint: a move by a player meant to deceive an opposing player; used by a *ball carrier* to make a *defender* think the ball carrier is going to *dribble*, *pass* or *shoot* in a certain direction when he is not.

Far post: the *goalpost* furthest from the ball.

Field: the rectangular area where soccer *matches* are played.

FIFA: Federation Internationale de Football Association — the official governing body of international soccer since 1904 which established the *World Cup* tournament; helps set and revise rules of the game, called the *17 Laws*.

FIFA World Cup: a solid gold statue given to the champion of each *World Cup* tournament to keep for the next 4 years.

Flick header: a player's use of his head to *deflect* the ball.

Foot trap: a player's use of the bottom or sides of his shoe to control a rolling or low-bouncing ball.

Football: name for soccer everywhere except in the U.S.; also, what American's call their popular team sport which evolved from soccer and *rugby*.

Formation: the arrangement into positions of players on the *field*; for example, a *4-3-3* formation places 4 *defenders*, 3 *midfielders* and 3 *forwards* on the field.

Forward line: the 3 or 4 *forwards* who work together to try and score *goals*; consists of two *wingers* and 1 or 2 *strikers*.

Forward pass: a *pass* made towards the opposition's *goal*.

Forwards: the 3 or 4 players on a team who are responsible for most of a team's scoring; they play in front of the rest of their team where they can take most of its *shots*; *strikers* and *wingers*.

Foul: a violation of the rules for which an *official* assesses a *free kick*.

4-2-4: a *formation* that consists of 4 *defenders*, 2 *midfielders* and 4 *forwards*.

4-3-3: a *formation* that consists of 4 *defenders*, 3 *midfielders* and 3 *forwards*; the most common formation used by teams.

4-4-2: a *formation* that consists of 4 *defenders*, 4 *midfielders* and 2 *forwards*.

Free kick: a kick awarded to a player for a *foul* committed by the opposition; the player kicks a stationary ball without any opposing players within 10 feet of him.

Front header: the striking of a ball in the air by a player's forehead; the most common type of *header*.

Front tackle: an attempt by a *defender* to kick the ball away from an *attacker* by approaching him from a head-on position.

Fullbacks: see *Defensemen*.

Goal: a ball that crosses the *goal line* between the *goalposts* and below the *crossbar* for which a *point* is awarded; also, the 8-foot high, 24-foot wide structure consisting of two *posts*, a *crossbar* and a *net* into which all goals are scored.

Goal area: the rectangular area 20 yards wide by 6 yards deep in front of each *goal* from which all *goal kicks* are taken; inside this area, it is illegal for opposing players to *charge* a *goalie* not holding the ball.

Goal kick: a type of restart where the ball is kicked from inside the *goal area* away from the *goal*; awarded to the *defending team* when a ball that crossed the *goal line* was last touched by a player on the *attacking team*.

Goal line: the *field* boundary running along its width at each end; also called the *end line*; runs right across the front of the *goal*; the line which a ball must completely cross for a goal to be scored.

Goalie: see *Goalkeeper*.

Goalkeeper or *goalie*: the player positioned directly in front of the *goal* who tries to prevent *shots* from getting into the *net* behind him; the only player allowed to use his hands and arms, though only within the *penalty area*.

Goalmouth: the front opening to each *goal*.

Goalposts: the two vertical beams located 24 feet apart which extend 8 feet high to form the sides of a *goal* and support the *crossbar*.

Hacking: kicking an opponent's legs.

Halfback: see *Midfielder*.

Halftime: the *intermission* between the 2 *periods* or *halves* of a game.

Halves: see *Periods*.

Hand ball: a *foul* where a player touches the ball with his hand or arm; the opposing team is awarded a *direct free kick*.

Hat trick: 3 or more *goals* scored in a game by a single player.

Header: the striking of a ball in the air by a player's head.

Hook: the curved trajectory of a ball due to spin imparted on it by a kicker, such as in a *banana kick*.

IFAB: International Football Association Board — the organization consisting of 4 British soccer organizations and *FIFA* that approves all changes in the official international rules of soccer called the *17 Laws*.

In bounds: when a ball is within the boundaries of the *field*, having not completely crossed a *sideline* or *goal line*.

In play: when a ball is within the boundaries of the *field* and play has not been stopped by the *referee*.

Indirect free kick: a kick awarded to a player for a less-serious *foul* committed by the opposition; the player kicks a stationary ball without any opposing players within 10 feet of him; a *goal* can only be scored on this kick after the ball has touched another player.

Injury time: time added to the end of any *period* according to the *referee's* judgment of time lost due to player injuries or intentional stalling by a team.

Instep drive: a straight *shot* taken with the instep of a player's foot; usually the most powerful and accurate of shots.

Intermission: the 5-minute rest period between *periods* of a game.

Juggling: keeping a ball in the air with any part of the body besides the hands or arms; used for practice and developing coordination.

Jules Rimet Trophy: the trophy given to the *World Cup* winner between 1930 and 1970, after which it was permanently retired.

Kickoff: the method of starting a game or restarting it after each *goal*; a player *passes* the ball forward to a teammate from the *center spot*.

Laws of the Game: the 17 main rules for soccer established by *FIFA*.

Lead pass: a *pass* sent ahead of a moving teammate to arrive at a location at the same time he does.

League: an alliance of teams that organizes sporting competition.

Linesmen: the 2 *officials* who assist the *referee* in making his decisions; they monitor the *sidelines* and *goal lines* to determine when a ball goes *out of bounds* and they carry a flag to signal their observations.

Linkmen: see *Midfielders*.

Loft or lob: a high-arcing kick.

Man-to-man: a type of *defense* where each *defender* is assigned to *mark* a different *forward* from the other team; the most common type of defense for national-level teams.

Marking: guarding a player to prevent him from advancing the ball towards the *net*, making an easy *pass* or getting the ball from a teammate.

Match: a soccer game.

Midfield: the region of the *field* near the *midfield line*; the area controlled by the *midfielders*.

Midfield anchor: See *Defensive midfielder*.

Midfield line or *center line*: a line that divides the *field* in half along its width.

Midfielders: the 2, 3 or 4 players who link together the *offensive* and *defensive* functions of a team; they play behind their *forwards*.

MISL: Major Indoor Soccer League — started in the U.S. in 1977 playing games of 6 players per side in modified hockey rinks covered by artificial turf; became the *MSL* in 1990.

Mismatch: when a particular *offensive player* is far superior to the *defender marking* him.

MLS: Major League Soccer — the new U.S. outdoor *league* scheduled to begin play in the Spring of 1995.

MSL: Major Soccer League — a U.S. indoor *league* which formed in 1990 from the *MISL* and folded in 1992.

NASL: North American Soccer League — an outdoor *league* formed in the U.S. in 1967 that attracted great international players including *Pelé* and huge audiences to the U.S. in the 1970s; folded in 1985.

National team: a team consisting of the best players in a country chosen to represent it in international competitions such as the *World Cup*.

NCAA: National Collegiate Athletic Association — governs and organizes sports at the collegiate level; has its own soccer committee.

Near post: the *goalpost* closest to the ball.

Net: hemp, jute or nylon cord draped over the frame of the *goal* and extending behind it; also used to refer to the goal itself.

NPSL: National Professional Soccer League — a U.S. indoor *league* that plays its games in a modified hockey rink, much like the former *MISL*; plays by non-traditional rules to create a faster-paced, higher-scoring game; also, a different league by the same name that played in the 1960s, merging with another league to form the *NASL*.

Obstruction: when a *defensive player*, instead of going after the ball, uses his body to prevent an *offensive player* from *playing* it.

Offense: the function of trying to *score goals*.

Offensive player: see *Attacker*.

Offensive team: see *Attacking team*.

Official game clock: the clock that the *referee* carries with him on the *field* so he can signal when each *half* is over; does not stop during the game, even when play does.

Officials: the *referee* and 2 *linesmen* who work together to make sure the game is played according to the rules of soccer; responsible for stopping and restarting play, keeping track of the score and the time remaining and citing violations of the rules, called *fouls*; they wear uniforms that distinguish them from the players on both teams.

Offside: a violation called when a player in an *offside position* receives a *pass* from a teammate; an *indirect free kick* is awarded to the non-offending team.

Offside position: an *attacking player* positioned so that fewer than 2 opposing *defensive players* (usually the *goalie* and 1 other *defender*) are between him and the *goal* he is attacking; a player is not offside if he is exactly even with one or both of these defensive players.

On defense: describes a team that does not have *possession* of the ball.

On offense: describes a team in *possession* of the ball.

On-side: the opposite of *offside*.

Open: describes an *attacking player* who does not have anyone *marking* him.

Out of bounds: when a ball is outside the boundaries of the *field*, having completely crossed a *sideline* or *goal line*.

Out of play: when a ball is outside the boundaries of the *field* or play has been stopped by the *referee*.

Outlet passes: when a *goaltender* or *defender passes* the ball from close to his own *goal* toward the other team's goal; used to start a *counterattack*.

Overlap: when a *winger* moves away from the *sideline* towards the center of the *field* to *create space* for a teammate to advance the ball undefended along the side of the field.

Overtime: the extra *periods* played after a *regulation game* ends *tied*; used in collegiate and championship international *matches* to determine a winner.

Passing: when a player kicks the ball to his teammate; used to move the ball closer to the opposing *goal*, to keep the ball away from an opponent or to give the ball to a player who is in a better position to *score*.

Penalty: short for *penalty kick*; also, a punishment given by the *referee* for a violation of the rules.

Penalty arc: a circular arc whose center is the *penalty spot* and extends from the top of the *penalty area*; designates an area that opposing players are not allowed to enter prior to a *penalty kick*.

Penalty area: a rectangular area 44 yards wide by 18 yards deep with its long edge on the *goal line*; the *goalkeeper* may use his hands to block or control the ball only within this area.

Penalty kick: see *Penalty shot*.

Penalty shot or *penalty kick*: a kick taken from the *penalty spot* by a player against the opposing *goalie* without any players closer than 10 yards away; awarded for the most severe rule violations and those committed by the *defense* within its own *penalty area*; also taken in a *tiebreaker* to decide a *match*.

Penalty spot: the small circular spot located 12 yards in front of the center of the *goal line* from which all *penalty kicks* are taken; positioned at the center of the *penalty arc*.

Penetrate: to advance the ball *behind* opposing *defenders* (between them and their *goal*).

Periods: the segments of time into which a game is divided; a *regulation game* played by adults consists of two 45-minutes *halves*.

Pitch: a British term for soccer *field*.

Play: to *trap*, *dribble*, kick or *head* the ball.

Play on: a term used by *referees* to indicate that no *foul* or stoppage is to be called; used by referees when applying the *Advantage Rule*.

Playoff: a tournament that takes place after a season's schedule has been completed; used to determine a champion.

Points: a team statistic indicating its degree of success, calculated as follows: 2 points for a win (3 in the 1994 World Cup), 1 point for a tie, 0 points for a loss; also, an individual statistic for a player, calculated by totaling 2 points for each *goal* and 1 point for each *assist*.

Possession: control of the ball.

Post: *goalpost* or the area near it.

Professional foul: a *foul* committed intentionally, usually by a *defender* on an *attacker* just outside the defender's *penalty area*; used to prevent a *scoring opportunity* without incurring a *penalty shot*.

Push pass: when a player pushes the ball with the inside of his foot to a teammate.

Qualifying Draw: the division of teams into groups for *World Cup qualifying matches*, held 2 years before *The Draw*.

Qualifying matches: games played in the 2 years preceding the *World Cup* to determine which teams participate in the tournament.

Receiver: a player who gets a *pass* from a teammate.

Red card: a playing card-sized card that a *referee* holds up to signal a player's removal from the game; the player's team must play the rest of the game *shorthanded*; presented for violent behavior or multiple rule infractions (two *yellow cards* = one red card).

Referee: the chief *official*; he makes all final decisions, acts as *timekeeper*, calls all *fouls* and starts and stops play.

Regular season: the schedule of games set before the season; consists of all games played before a *playoff* or tournament is held.

Regulation game: two completed *periods* of a game, prior to any *overtime* or *tiebreaker*.

Round: a stage of a tournament at which teams compete; the *World Cup* tournament has 5 main rounds.

Rugby: an offshoot from soccer started in the early 1800s; rugby players are allowed to pick up the ball with their hands and run with it, and also make full contact with each other whether going after the ball or not.

Save: the act of a *goalkeeper* in blocking or stopping a *shot* that would have gone into the *goal* without his intervention.

Scissors kick: see *Bicycle kick*.

Score: to put the ball into the *net* for a *goal*; also, the tally of goals for each team playing in a game.

Scorers: players who score *goals*.

Scoring opportunity: a situation where a team stands a good chance of scoring a *goal*.

Screening: see *Shielding*.

Set play: a planned strategy that a team uses when a game is restarted with a *free kick*, *penalty kick*, *corner kick*, *goal kick*, *throw-in* or *kickoff*.

Shielding or *screening*: a technique used by a *ball carrier* to protect the ball from a *defender* closely *marking* him; the ball carrier keeps his body between the ball and the *defender.*

Shinguards: pads that strap onto a player's lower leg to protect the shins should he or she be kicked there.

Shooting: when a player kicks the ball at the opponent's *net* in an attempt to score a *goal*.

Shorthanded: a team playing with less than its full complement of 11 players.

Shot: a ball kicked or headed by a player at the opponent's *net* in an attempt to score a *goal*.

Shoulder charge: minimal shoulder-to-shoulder contact by a *defender* against a *ball carrier*; the only contact allowed by the rules unless a defender touches the ball first.

Shutout: preventing the opposition from scoring any *goals* in a game; for example, a score of 2-0 or 4-0; *goalies* are often credited with shutouts because they did not allow any goals to get past them.

Side tackle: an attempt by a *defender* to redirect the ball slightly with his foot away from a *ball carrier* running in the same direction.

Sideline or *touchline*: a line that runs along the length of the *field* on each side.

Single elimination: a type of tournament where a single loss eliminates a team from the tournament.

Sliding tackle: an attempt by a *defender* to take the ball away from a *ball carrier* by sliding on the ground feet-first into the ball.

Small-sided game: a *match* played with fewer than 11 players per side.

Square pass: a *pass* made by a player to a teammate running alongside him.

Starter: a player who is on the *field* to play at the start of a game; a team usually makes its best players starters.

Steal: when a player takes the ball away from an opposing player.

Stopper: the *defender* that *marks* the best *scorer* on the *attacking team*, often the opposition's *striker*; exists only in a *man-to-man defense*.

Striker: a team's most powerful and best-scoring *forward* who plays towards the center of the *field*; also, the name of the *mascot* for the 1994 *World Cup*.

Substitution: replacement of one player on the *field* with another player not on the field; *FIFA* rules allow only 2 substitutions per game.

Sudden death: a type of *overtime* where the first *goal* scored by a team ends the game and gives that team the victory; most overtime in soccer is <u>not</u> sudden death.

Sweeper: the *defender* that plays closest to his own *goal behind* the rest of the *defenders*; a team's last line of *defense* in front of the *goalkeeper*.

Tackling: the act of taking the ball away from a player by kicking or stopping it with one's feet; only a minimal amount of shoulder-to-shoulder contact, called a *charge*, is permitted to knock the *ball carrier* off balance.

Territory: the half of the *field* which a team defends.

Thigh trap: when a player uses his thigh to slow down and control a ball in the air.

3-on-1 break: a type of *break* with 3 *attacking players* against only 1 *defensive player*.

3-on-2 break: a type of *break* with 3 *attacking players* against 2 d*efensive players*.

Through pass: a *pass* sent to a teammate to get him the ball *behind* his *defender*; used to *penetrate* a line of defenders.

113

Throw-in: a type of restart where a player throws the ball from behind his head with two hands while standing with both feet on the ground behind a *sideline*; taken by a player opposite the team that last touched the ball before it went *out of bounds* across a sideline.

Tie game: when two teams have scored the same number of *goals* in a *match*; if the game ends tied, it is a *draw*.

Tiebreaker: a way to choose the winner of a *match* when teams are tied after *overtime*; in *FIFA* tournament play, a series of *penalty kicks* are taken by players from both teams, and the team that scores on more of them is declared the winner.

Timekeeper: the job of the *referee*, who keeps track of the official time to notify teams and fans when each *period* is completed.

Timeout: an official break in the action of a sport; the rules of soccer do not allow for any timeouts; timeouts for television advertising breaks are permitted by *NCAA* collegiate rules.

Touchline: see *Sideline*.

Trailing: running behind another player.

Trap: when a player uses his body to slow down and control a moving ball, most often using his chest, thighs or feet.

Turnover: the loss of *possession* of the ball.

2-on-1 break: a type of *break* with 2 *attacking players* against 1 *defensive player*.

Two-way midfielder: the versatile *midfielder* most responsible for organizing play in the *midfield* area; often a team's energetic leader.

Unsportsmanlike conduct: rude behavior.

USSF: United States Soccer Federation — organization formed in 1913 to govern soccer in America; America's link to *FIFA*, providing soccer rules and guidelines to players, *referees* and spectators nationwide.

USYSA: United States Youth Soccer Association — the official Youth Division of the *USSF* and the largest youth soccer organization in the U.S.; organizes and administers youth league competitions, establishes rules and guidelines, and holds clinics and workshops to support players, coaches and *referees*.

Venue: location where a sporting competition is held.

Volley: any ball kicked by a player when it is off the ground.

Wall: a line of 2 to 6 *defending players* pressed together shoulder-to-shoulder to protect their *goal* against a close *free kick*; creates a more difficult *shot* by reducing the amount of open goal area the kicker has to *shoot* at.

Wall pass: a *pass* by a *ball carrier* who sends the ball to a teammate, then runs *behind his own defender* and quickly receives a pass back; used to get a player past his defender without having to *dribble* by him; same as the "give-and-go" in basketball.

Win-draw-loss record: a summary of the outcomes of a team's *matches*; for example, a team with a 3-1-2 record has played 6 games and won 3, tied 1 and lost 2.

Wings or wingers: the outside *forwards* who play to the sides of the *strikers* and whose primary task is to provide them with accurate *crossing passes* so they can *shoot* at the *goal*; often the fastest players and best *dribblers* on a team.

World Cup: the international soccer competition held by *FIFA* every 4 years between the top professional teams in the world, pitting nation against nation; the most watched event in the world, attracting a television audience of over 3 billion viewers.

Yellow card: a playing card-sized card that a *referee* holds up to warn a player for dangerous or *unsportsmanlike* behavior; also called a *caution*; 2 yellow cards in one game earns a player an automatic *red card*, signaling his removal from the game.

Zone: a type of *defense* that assigns each *defender* to a particular area in front of or around his team's *goal* in which he is responsible for *marking* any *attacker* that enters; often used in youth league games but rarely in professional competition.

INDEX

Bolded page numbers indicate a photograph, diagram or table.

E

F

G

H

I

J

K

L

M

N

O

P

Q

R

S

T

U

V

W

Y

Z

OFFICIALS' HAND SIGNALS

REFEREE SIGNALS

CAUTION or EXPULSION:
Referee holds *yellow card*
or *red card* above his head.

PLAY ON / ADVANTAGE:
Referee indicates with his
hands that the *Advantage
Rule* applies and play
should continue.

DIRECT FREE KICK:
Referee points in
direction of kick.

INDIRECT FREE KICK: Referee raises his hand until ball is kicked and touched by another player.

GOAL KICK: Referee points to a corner of *goal area* from which kick is to be taken.

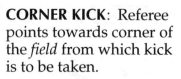

CORNER KICK: Referee points towards corner of the *field* from which kick is to be taken.

PENALTY KICK:
Referee points to
penalty mark from
which kick is to be
taken.

LINESMEN SIGNALS

THROW-IN: *Linesman*
holds the flag out to his
side, pointing in the
direction the throw is to be
taken.

CORNER KICK:
Linesman points
his flag at *corner
area* from which
kick is to be taken.

OFFSIDE: Linesman points his flag straight up above his head to signal *offside* violation to the referee.

OFFSIDE LOCATION: After linesman signals offside, he then shows location of infraction by holding his flag out in front of him — flag held <u>high</u> indicates infraction occurred at far side of the *field*, <u>middle</u> = center of field, <u>low</u> = side of field nearest to him.

GOAL KICK: Linesman points his flag at *goal area* from which kick is to be taken.

SUBSTITUTION: Linesman signals to the referee by holding his flag overhead with both hands.

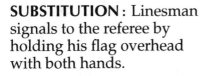

1994 WORLD CUP SCHEDULE

	GROUPS A and B			GROUPS C and D			GROUPS E and F		
JUNE	Pasadena Calif. Rose Bowl	Palo Alto Calif. Stanford Stadium	Pontiac Mich. Silverdome	Chicago Ill. Soldier Field	Foxboro Mass. Foxboro Stadium	Dallas Tex. Cotton Bowl	E. Rutherford N.J. Giants Stadium	Orlando Fla. Citrus Bowl	Washington D.C. R.F.K. Stadium
17				Germany v. Bolivia		Spain v. South Korea			
18	Colombia v. Romania		United States v. Switzerland				Italy v. Ireland		
19	Cameroon v. Sweden							Belgium v. Morocco	Norway v. Mexico
20		Brazil v. Russia							Netherlands v. Saudi Arabia
21				Germany v. Spain	Argentina v. Greece	Nigeria v. Bulgaria			
22	United States v. Colombia		Romania v. Switzerland						
23					South Korea v. Bolivia		Italy v. Norway		
24		Brazil v. Cameroon	Sweden v. Russia					Mexico v. Ireland	
25					Argentina v. Nigeria		Saudi Arabia v. Morocco	Belgium v. Netherlands	
26	United States v. Romania	Switzerland v. Colombia		Bulgaria v. Greece					
27				Bolivia v. Spain		Germany v. South Korea			
28		Russia v. Cameroon	Brazil v. Sweden				Ireland v. Norway		Italy v. Mexico
29								Morocco v. Netherlands	Belgium v. Saudi Arabia
30					Greece v. Nigeria	Argentina v. Bulgaria			

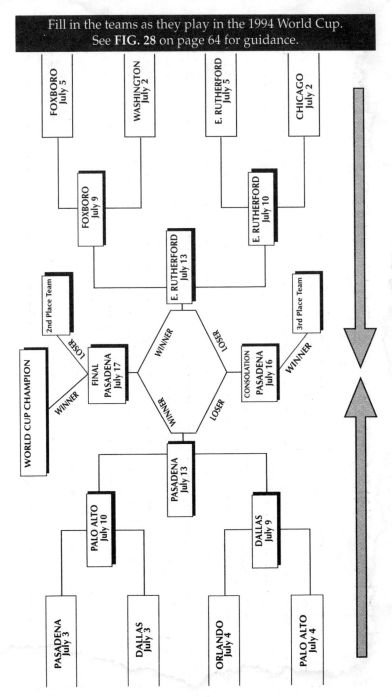

127

NOTES